THINKING FINANCIALLY

PRACTICAL SKILLS OF
A CORPORATE STRATEGIST

RYUHO OKAWA

IRH Press

Contents

CHAPTER TWO

Q&A Session

Assessing Whether an Investment Is Effective, Active and Acceptable

Preface

After graduating university, I went through an age of discipline as a person in the secular world. I was a financial elite of a trading company that regularly ranked in the top 10 on a worldwide scale and which contributed to one to two percent of Japan's GDP.

I was an international financial genius who was said to be unrivaled ten years before and ten years after me. My career advancement as becoming both a senior management executive and a corporate strategist was unprecedented. I renounced the world and became independent to become a religious leader. I even required approval from the vice president when leaving the company. Furthermore, the impact at the time was so large that my bosses in management were knocked off the fast track.

I thought I had gotten rid of my memories regarding my trading company days. The reason Happy Science has become a religious organization that represents Japan and was able to expand its activities worldwide was definitely due to my financial knowledge, experience and way of thinking as a financial expert.

In these pages I have revealed the financial thinking of a professional as a concept of the Faculty of Successful Management at Happy Science University[*].

Ryuho Okawa
Founder and CEO of Happy Science Group
Founder of Happy Science University
August 28, 2014

---

[*] Happy Science University: a religious institution for higher education established by Happy Science. Opened in April 2015.

Chapter One

Thinking Financially
~ Practical Skills of a Corporate Strategist ~

Lecture given on July 4, 2014
Happy Science General Headquraters

1

Understanding Financial Concepts

Describing finances from the viewpoint of Practical management

Today, I would like to speak about an element of practical business management, specifically related to finances.

As jobs today have split up into many elements, it will be too difficult to speak about everything. It would be great if you were to gain a broader understanding of what financial way of thinking is from this lecture. This information is necessary for anyone who is in management, those who aim to be a management executive, the business elite and even students who are interested in studying management.

Finances will not come easy just by listening to this lecture. However, at the very least you will find that *knowledge is power* and the knowledge will become a resource for your thinking and a clue for your personal research. During my lay working years, I was part of the finance department. This is why finance, as a practical process of this world, is something I am most familiar with.

As we are a religion, there are many differences compared to a company. Nevertheless, instead of getting caught up in the differences between a religion and a company, I would like to generalize and teach a universal scope of financial concepts.

Thinking financially is a requirement for Top management

This is not a subject that one can learn easily, nor is it easy to teach. Many company CEOs, in spiritual terms, just follow the guide of their guardian spirits. In worldly terms, they rely largely on their intuition to make financial decisions. The effect of their personalities can be widely seen within their finances. By analyzing the root cause, we can see the person's personality and habitual actions will influence his financial thinking. Of course, the biggest results will come from the top person in charge.

Whenever I speak about management, people who are in management tend to dislike what I have to say. The management executives, who are called *daikokuten* or Angels of Wealth* in our organization, will often say, "I'm always being scolded," or "I'm being told this again,"

---

* Angels of Wealth: people who are passionate financial supporters of a Buddhist organization.

or "Master always says that CEOs, as a whole, are like *tengus* who like to boast and always lack in terms of self-reflection. I'm also annoyed about how he keeps repeating himself." However, usually they are a conceited existence, so they all tend to forget if I don't repeat myself. This is why what I say is important.

In business, the personality and thought patterns of the top executive will affect all. On a larger scope, a nation is the same. There's a Chinese saying, "A nation is founded and destroyed by one person."[*] Therefore, the concept of having a single person affecting the rest can be applied to a country.

There's an idea in economics that splits it into macroeconomics and microeconomics. However, it's true that on a national level, not everything is done purely for profit. This is why there are many viewpoints that enter the equation. Nevertheless, on a larger scale, countries too can become larger or smaller and can fail or go bankrupt with just the top person himself.

Every head of a company will require knowledge in finance. This is why I would like for these people to have a basic concept of finance. But when the company grows to a certain size, the top person won't be able to do everything. The finance department must be able

[*] The words of Su Xun [1009-1066], a writer during the Northern Song Dynasty and one of the Eight Great Writers of Tang and Song Dynasties.

to function as a company strategist or a staff section — similar to the military definition of staff — to support the top person. Otherwise, the company can't be maintained.

There's a multitude of recent businesses that are started by CEOs and management by developing a certain technology. I believe this category comprises over half of the newer businesses. There are cases where they create or invent something that never existed before. Once discovered, they spread this or sell it in order to build up a company. There are a lot of technological entrepreneurs and managers. They can understand the financial situation of their company and do well while it's still small. But as the company grows, they become unable to see their financial situation. This is the key point to whether their company can keep growing and also the key point to whether their company will go bankrupt. This is why they must hire a professional or somebody with specialized knowledge and experience once their company grows beyond a certain size. Otherwise, their company will go bankrupt if they aim to make their company grow further.

Separating ideas between Finance and accounting

What many CEOs with a technological background and CEOs with a sales background can't comprehend is that there is a real possibility for a company to go into a black-ink bankruptcy. They are completely in the black in their single-year figures or in the assets and debts sections on their balance sheet* but somehow, they go bankrupt. The reason for this is that they could not understand finance.

Those who center their thoughts on technological developments believe that money is a necessity. However, they believe that if they can sell their products and the balance is in surplus, there is no way their company can go bust. Contrary to their belief, sometimes the company goes under and this is what they do not understand. They do not believe that they will go bust because their sales are greater than their expenses and they have positive revenue, yet the company goes bust.

CEOs with a technological background will not understand this. In addition, CEOs with a sales background, especially the experts in their specialized fields who applied their selling abilities to start a company, will not understand this concept most of the time. CEOs who marketed pre-existing products or services and grew their sales numbers are unable to grow a company above a certain size or end up bankrupting the company. This happens because they do not possess a financial viewpoint.

Black-ink bankruptcy occurs frequently. There are many companies that go bust because they are always in the red and never in the black. Therefore, being in the black is in itself a great feat. A company that cannot sell its inventory even while spending resources on it will go bust. But whether the company goes bust when their goods are selling depends on whether the company actually knows about its finances. A company which does not go under in terms of its accounting can go under because of its finances [or in terms of cash flow]. This is the point that separates finance and accounting.

Reasons for black-ink bankruptcies

Mr. Kazuo Inamori[†] often says that maximizing sales and keeping expenses to the minimum makes maximum profit, in terms of accounting. What he says is easy to

---

[*]Balance sheet: a statement of the assets, liabilities and capital of a business at a particular point in time (i.e. end of a financial year).

[†]Kazuo Inamori [1932-2022]: a Japanese business owner. The founder of Kyocera Corporation (a multinational electronics and ceramics manufacturer based in Kyoto, Japan) and KDDI Corporation (one of the leading telecommunication companies in Japan). In 2010, he was asked by the Japanese government to restructure Japan Airlines by the Japanese government. He succeeded in doing so and retired after that.

understand. He says, "Maximize sales and minimize expenses. Roughly speaking, the difference between them is the profit. The important thing is to increase the difference." With these words, almost all employees can understand that they need to increase sales and keep costs down.

In practical terms, they can try to gain more customers to utilize their services or buy their products; meanwhile they can keep their own spending minimized, which produces a company that can create profit. This is Inamori-style management in a nutshell.

However, there is a hole in this theory. This thinking is correct in terms of accounting, but it is not enough in terms of finance. This is because a company can go bankrupt though it's in the black. I would like to explain why this kind of failure exists.

Companies sell their products. When sales representatives want to make a sure sell of their products, they often ask or force their long-standing clients to "just leave the products there for the time being." In technical terms, this is registered under *accounts receivable*[*]. Accounts receivable are allocated as assets, which contribute to a positive balance. However, accounts receivable only become cash when the company collects its receivables.

---

[*] Account receivable: a trusted purchase by individuals or corporations which is wed to another entity in exchange for goods or services delivered or used, but not yet paid for.

Literature from the Edo period depicts comical instances regarding how business owners try to hide and "get through another year," so they are not caught by bill collectors on December 31st. An author made money by writing a funny book that researched how to surprise the collectors and make them go home. The book gives examples of bill collectors not being able to collect money at the end of the year, such as, "the owner pretended to be crazy when collectors came" or "the owner cut off a chicken's head and made it run, which scared off the bill collectors."

The point is not to run short of money

Once an object is sold, a contract is established. As the contract is set up, we now have an accounts receivable. As the creditor, there is a credit that exists. However, unless the credit is collected, this does not become part of the income. What if you could not collect this credit before December 31st, but needed to make a payment on December 31st? What would happen?

As an example, if there was an account receivable that was valued at 120 million yen [1.2 million dollars at ¥100=$1. Same rate applies throughout this book] but there was already a cost of 100 million yen [one million dollars] for resources that had been incurred, you must be able to pay 100 million yen by the end of the year. If you can't pay, you would not be able to have the resources delivered to you after that. If you want to continue making products in the following year, you must be able to pay 100 million yen before the end of the year.

So you try to collect the outstanding account receivable worth 120 million yen, but the president of the client company has disappeared and cannot be reached. He could have left for an end-of-the-year or New Year's vacation but anyway, he cannot be found. He could have run off to Hawaii, he could have run off to Yufuin* in Kyushu. Anyway, his whereabouts are unknown. You frantically search for him, but you cannot track him down. Like this, if the president runs away, the account receivable cannot be collected.

From an accounting point of view, you are profitable by 20 million yen [200,000 dollars] but, in reality, you are 120 million yen short in cash. Out of this, 100 million yen must be paid out, however, the amount could not be received in cash. The 20 million yen that is supposed to count as profit could not be received in cash, either. Even if you plan out the new year with the 120 million yen, as the money is not yet paid in, the situation occurs where you're not able to pay wages by the end of January.

This is the point that must be thought out by thinking financially. The balance of payment must be exact in terms of cash flow. It must be balanced out exactly. In finance, this is the reason why there is a method of creating financial statements for daily, weekly, monthly and annual time frames. With this, you can look at your numbers from a range of three months, six months, a year or few years.

When there is not enough funds, you are short on funds. It is important to never be short on capital. Black-ink bankruptcy occurs because of capital shortage. In other words, you don't have the funds to make the payment. If you issue a check and it becomes dishonored[†] due to insufficient funds, the company will lose credit from the bank and will no longer do business with you. Your company can go bankrupt from losing credit. In this way, you can go bankrupt while having a positive balance.

---

[*] Yufuin: a famous tourist spot in Japan, known for hot springs. Also the location of one of the main temples of Happy Science.

[†] Dishonored check: a check that cannot be processed because the writer of the check has insufficient funds.

You should not valuate assets at face value alone

There are also other ways, besides black-ink bankruptcies, in which a company can go bankrupt.

Bonds, stocks and securities are classified as assets. They exist as assets but their values may depreciate, causing the book value to become different from the actual value or even of no worth. However, a CEO who does not understand finance may feel relieved that the company is profitable by taking these things at face value [acquired value] and looking at the balance sheet. Looking at just the numbers based on book value, he believes that his company is profitable and raises wages, employs more people and gives out bonuses. Perhaps believing that a foreign government bond has a good yield, the company buys the bond but the bond crashes. There are cases where the company will, in truth, be in the red.

If he sells that bond after it has crashed, the losses will become very obvious. But if the bond wasn't sold, nobody would know for sure.

This is what happened when Yamaichi Securities[*] went bankrupt. They used *tobashi* schemes[†]. If you sell securities with unrealized losses, that will be recorded as a "red" in the profit-and-loss statement, so you do not want to do that. In order to hide this, some companies transfer these losses to subsidiary companies and other organizations in order to hide the fact that they were in the red. Even the company's top personnel can be deceived by this method, not knowing that these things have occurred.

Another way is when one believes that they own assets, but in reality they are unable to sell these assets. This is why believing that you are OK because you have assets can be a mistake.

Recently, there was a Japanese drama called *The Roosevelt Games.* Dramas based around businesses are sometimes a little helpful.

The Roosevelt Games follows a business in the red. The bank, as a condition to continue lending, pressures the company to dismantle its baseball team. The bank says that it is of the utmost luxury for a failing company to hold onto its baseball team. The baseball field is an *idle asset.* The field is large. The baseball team does not work all day; rather, they work until noon and play in the afternoon.

The company allows for this to happen and lets itself be engrossed in the results of the baseball team and neglects management duties. This is a sign that the

---

*Yamaichi Securities: one of the largest Japanese securities trading firms which went bankrupt in 1997. The firm went bankrupt due to management failure that occurred after the cover-up incident. See p.98.

† Tobashi scheme: hiding losses off the company's balance sheet by holding onto and shifting unrealized securities losses to a third party.

company will go bust. The bank tells the company to get rid of its baseball team, which is natural for a bank to say. However, if the company takes pride in its baseball team, selling the field and breaking up the team will mean the end of the company. This is how the company sees the situation. It seems as if a company tradition is being wiped out.

Banks often tell companies to sell off their idle assets. This issue is related to company's investments and operations, but I will not expand too much on this idea, since I do not want to get into a specialized topic.

Finances of a company correspond to The circulation of blood in the human body

Ultimately, finance corresponds to the circulation of blood in the human body. People die if blood does not circulate well. In businesses, blood is money. Without the circulation of money, the company will perish. Although it may seem circulation is good because the bank is loaning you money now, once the loans end or are collected, the circulation of money will stop.

When enjoying a regular economy or growth similar to Japan's past [post-war growth from the 1960s to 1980s before the bubble burst in Japan], business will continue to grow as long as the management is not too sloppy. Banks will feel safe and will continue to loan out short-term loans of about one year, with rollovers[*].

A long-term loan could be three, five or seven-year loan. Money cannot be collected for businesses like factories unless they take out a long–term loan. Therefore, although interest rates will be higher, there are companies who are able to manage themselves well due to long-term loans. If the business is on track, this is fine, but circumstances can suddenly change.

In the burst of the Japanese bubble in the 90s, land prices rapidly dropped. This was caused by the Miyazawa administration.[†] The plan was a project to boost assets, however in reality, land prices dropped.

Imagine if that were to happen now. Usually, banks loan money with land, factories and buildings as collateral. Factories do not amount to much, but the land they are built upon including the building is given an assessed value for calculating collateral. This collateral can bring a loan amount that is 70-80% of the valuation. The loan could be 700 to 800 million yen [seven to eight million dollars] if the factory and land were valued at one billion

---

[*] Rollover: to replace an older loan term with a new term once the loan term comes to an end.

[†] Miyazawa administration: a Japanese cabinet, led by Prime Minister Kiichi Miyazawa, that lasted from November 1991 to August 1993. Miyazawa was a former official at the Ministry of Finance.

yen [10 million dollars]. If land prices constantly rose, the actual value of current real estate could turn into two or three billion yen [20 or 30 million dollars]. In the 1980s, banks were lax. They encouraged companies to buy more land and add more factories, eventually leading to unnecessary assets using their loan.

Once the bubble burst, banks were required to clean up their finances. Each branch had to meet their numbers in loan collections. They all started asking companies to pay their debt and began collecting their loans. When this happened, companies that thought they were in the clear suddenly lost funds and business owners became aghast. There were many companies that folded during this time.

A Japanese drama series called *Hanzawa Naoki** became popular last year. The author was a former Mitsubishi Bank employee who worked there until he was around 32. The period he worked there was probably when the bubble burst. Essentially, companies go under when banks recover the loan amount.

If a company is listed on the stock exchange, it can raise funds from its own stock. However, if the company is still privately owned and its bank loans dry up, that

---

* Hanzawa Naoki: a Japanese TV drama based on a popular novel of the same title. The drama depicts Naoki Hanzawa, who started working for a major bank near the end of the bubble period (beginning of 1990s), overcoming many pressure situations and setbacks thrown at him by people inside and outside the bank, as well as by other organizations.

company will occasionally get a loan from consumer-lending facilities in order to raise funds. They must borrow at a higher interest rate in order to repay the debt.

When this happens, a *yakuza*-like debt collector may come around and scare the owner enough to have his whole family run away in the middle of the night. It is also true that companies who have had banks take back their loans won't be able to use their stock to raise funds for themselves. Therefore, companies can suddenly go under with reasons that have nothing to do with them. The risk management for these scenarios is also part of finance.

2

The Work of the Finance Department

The work of the accounting department In early stages of the company's progress

There seems to be some people who do not understand the outline of finance, so I would like to delve into more detail. It is the norm to not have a finance department while a company is still small. It may have an accounting department, but some companies may not have this, either. If the company has a few to around 10 employees, there might only be one person responsible for general tasks with, perhaps, the title of section manager of general affairs in order to deal with banks.

Once the framework of the company becomes more structured, the accounting department separates itself from the general affairs department. Any aspect in relation with money becomes part of the accounting department. The accounting department will also handle things that the finance department of a large company would. Creating financial statements *, borrowing from and repaying banks,

---

*Financial statement: a formal record of the financial activities of a business presenting information of their performance and financial position within a certain time frame. A financial statement is fundamentally comprised of a balance sheet, profit and loss report and statement of cash flows.

fund management and payroll are also calculated here. The accounting department handles anything related to money.

The general affairs department handles all other general administrative tasks of the company as a whole. These include vehicle management, human resources, errands as well as equipment purchases and repairs. Roughly speaking, this is how general affairs and accounting departments are split.

Furthermore, the accounting department will split into accounting and finance as the company grows larger. The accounting department is responsible for financial statements which depicts the flow of company money at each reporting period. All income and loss, or whether the company finance is in the red or the black, are recorded as documents and examined daily. The accounting department checks to make sure there isn't any deception within the company accounts.

Negotiating with the bank is
The work of the finance department

One of the tasks of the finance department is to borrow money from the banks by negotiating with them. That is the work of the finance department. Borrowing money is, of course, the toughest task for the finance department. If the finance department does not yet exist, the CEO himself must go to the bank manager and ask for loans. The CEO himself must explain about the company and show its financial statements when negotiating with a bank. He would have to talk about what the company's situation is, how the business is running, how much money is required to start a factory, the development cost in order to complete a product and sell it on the market as well as how much profit can be expected. By talking about these topics, he would be able to talk about how much he needs in loans to continue with the business. Like this, the CEO may be required to negotiate with the banks.

Once the company grows, the finance department will begin to negotiate with banks. As I mentioned before, the finance department must look at the account activities, the incoming cash and outgoing payments and check that there are no funding shortages. When the payment date comes, whether at the end of the month, the 5th, 10th, 15th or 20th, you must check that your bank account has enough cash from the income that month.

A novice in the finance department will easily think they should borrow money to pay off expenses. Professional finance personnel do not think in this way. One method of doing this is to match up the date of payments with the date of deposits. For example, if you pay using a 3-month promissory note and are expecting 100 million yen [1 million dollars] to cash out in three months, you would make the day that the payment of expenses is due as the day your deposits [cash in] are set up. With this method, you have both deposits and withdrawals in one bank, so you will not be required to give extra effort. If the business required 100 million yen, you can pay by matching the payment date with the day you are receiving over 100 million yen in deposits. With this, you will no longer need to borrow 100 million yen. This phenomenon is like marriage, where you "marry" both the deposits and withdrawals together on the same date.

The finance department creates a financial plan

When the finance department makes a financial plan, they look at the large withdrawal payments and attempt to match the income date with these. They try as much as possible to match up the dates. The company will be in the red if the payments are due and there is a shortage of funds. This becomes a problem. They will need to borrow money. So instead of having this happen, in order to be able to pay off everything with their own means, they match up the dates of the withdrawals and the deposits.

In order to achieve this, the department must make a plan every day or every week. I have created a financial plan before, too, although it was for a branch office. In order to accurately tell the bank how much you require as a loan, you must be able to see how the company handles its funds as well as the company's income and expenses and come up with a financial plan. There will be some amount that you won't need to borrow, which you will be able to provide yourself.

As I have experienced with international business, I would like to explain this idea using foreign exchanges. For example, there might be an exchange between U.S. dollars and Japanese yen or an export and import of goods. There are exports and imports using dollars as well. If the day your deposits made from exports and the day your withdrawals are made from imports are on different days, for example, separated by 15 days, there will be a deficit worth 15 days. In this case, you must borrow from the bank and pay interest on the money.

This is wasteful. This is why you must match up the import and export days as much as possible. By marrying the two dates, you do not have to pay unnecessary interest. In foreign exchange, one can utilize this functionality. Most companies who build their business around import and export will utilize it.

When importing oil, if you were to make the day that the money you buy the oil goes out and the day the money you sell the oil comes in on the same day, you will not need to take out a loan from the bank and you will be able to make the payment on your own. The finance department will think like this.

Administrative departments such as Human resources, general affairs and secretaries

Earlier, I stated that as the company grows larger, finance and accounting split off. In addition, general affairs will also split into general affairs and human resources because general affairs alone will not be enough. General affairs will continue to fill up jobs such as errands and other general tasks. Human resources calculate items such as payroll, personnel residencies, total labor costs, medical insurance and condolence payments for families of the employees who have passed away.

The personnel who will actually bring the condolence payments to the family will most likely be someone in general affairs, but the person who does the calculations would be someone in human resources. This is how general affairs and human resources are split. Human resources also assess the employees and will decide who gets promoted and who does not. They also review or assess employee performance and differentiate salaries and bonuses between employees. Human resources must calculate how much employees must be paid in total. And thus, administrative departments are created.

If the company grows even larger, general affairs, human resources and also a secretarial department is created. The secretarial department has its ties to both general affairs and human resources. If the company gets even larger, there will be a secretary's office. These are an additional department, different from general affairs or human resources.

The secretarial department may be used by management executives and owners, however, they occasionally act by assisting sales. The secretarial department will add value to the general affairs team wherever they are lacking. Company presidents, vice presidents and senior directors all have information that may not be disclosed and are considered highly confidential. This information cannot be shown to regular employees. People who are trustworthy and can keep secrets, who will not backstab the company or steal from the company, are selected as secretarial department personnel.

There are support positions that are created for people at the top and the next rung down. Information that must not be shared must not be shared and information that must be shared must be shared. This is how an intelligence-like secretarial department similar to the covert forces is created.

This is roughly how the administrative departments are added.

Finance is the offense within the defense: Cash flow and fund management

Within the administrative departments lies the finance department. There is no doubt that the finance department and the accounting department function as the company's strategists. In terms of money, they must rid of their personal feelings and give their opinion. Loss of blood circulation will mean death, so like a doctor, the finance department must warn the company head if something is dangerous or if something is OK.

A functionality that finance has that accounting does not involves what I talked about earlier; keeping an eye on cash flow in and cash flow out, which is cash management. Another functionality that finance has which accounting does not is fund management or investment.

The company will make investments if it has some cash reserves. The finance department can also borrow money from the bank and invest it as well. With this investment they will see whether it will create value, in how much time, how much the total amount is and whether the investment will be worth going into debt for.

They can invest a portion of the profits into something that will be needed in the future, since they will have to pay more taxes if they post their entire profit amount. For instance, investment plans such as building factories or buying land for construction could be considered. Basically, the finance department draws up investment plans like that.

In this way, there are some tasks that the accounting department won't be able to handle. Accounting centers its strategy on defense. However, the finance department has aspects of offense within defense.

This is why finance must attack while defending. It is fair to say that whether rapidly growing companies from their technology development will survive or not depend on whether they have skillful finance personnel or not.

Shortcomings of CEOs with
A technological or sales background

Livedoor* went bankrupt after its aggregate market value amounted to 770 billion yen [7.7 billion dollars]. I believe its bankruptcy was due to the lack of skillful finance personnel. I feel people of Livedoor did not have an understanding of finance.

A CEO in the technology industry requires development funding. You can make a product if you have money, so you want money. However, there are many CEOs with a technological background who cannot tell the difference between debt and their own funds. You may still be a CEO even without this knowledge.

If the company employs between a few and 20 employees or so, then as long as the product sells, a person could act as the CEO even if he does not know the difference between debts and company funds. However, as a CEO, he must know the difference between debts and usable funds. All debts must be repaid. The money borrowed now will need to be paid back in a year, three years or five years. In order to be able to repay them, a

---

* Livedoor: a Japanese company that started up in 1999 as an Internet service provider. In 2002, Takafumi Horie, who was then 30 years old, took over as company head and rapidly expanded the business. He gained attention as a young business owner. But in 2006, Horie was arrested for securities fraud and was sentenced to imprisonment.

company must have people who will be able to balance the account.

Accounting frauds or other fraudulent events will occur if someone does not balance the account. A company will start window dressing their balance sheet in order to fool the bank; recording fictitious sales on account, hiding expenses well and various other tactics will get used. A company will fool the bank using such ways. The company will seek for a way to continue getting loans using fraudulent financial statements. However, this behavior will come into the open at some point. Either the company will get caught in violation of the Companies Act or will go bust by losing trust. These actions should be avoided.

In the long history of businesses, there are rarely companies that stay in business for 10 years and not have a money crisis. Almost all companies experience this. A person is not a true entrepreneur unless he is able to cross this pandemonium safely.

In terms of technology- or sales-oriented CEOs, there are cases where they do not know where the money is coming from or going to, nor do they know whether their own company is making money or losing money. However, CEOs must study subjects that they need to know.

Even if a company hires a specialist, the CEO should study aspects where he needs to study. If the CEO cannot understand the opinions of the specialist, he cannot be working as a good CEO. The CEO must understand enough, so that he can understand what the specialist is talking about. I believe CEOs must put in the time to study. The ideas I have mentioned in this section so far are what CEOs should know as the basics of finance.

Using strategic financial thinking To predict an era

Furthermore, I would like to talk about financial thinking that involves strategy of an even bigger concept. If the fiscal policy of the country changes and the trends change drastically, the business intelligence operations must be functioning, otherwise this may cause the company to go bust.

If, like the Miyazawa Cabinet, the government says they will double the assets of the people while in reality they implement a policy where assets are negated, then unexpected results will come forth. Whether the Miyazawa administration understood this effect is yet unknown. There is an opinion that suggests he knew the act would cause the assets to be negated, yet implemented the plan anyways. With this policy, they claimed that the salary of an individual could buy him a house in Tokyo. This would mean the price of land would drop rapidly.

If land were too expensive to purchase with one's salary, he would have to lower the cost of land by force in order to meet the policy. People who were working in banks or people who had ever borrowed money from banks would know the impact of forcefully dropping the cost of land. If a person who did not know this had decided on this policy, it would be a catastrophic incident. The Miyazawa administration had reduced the property value of the people of Japan. A lot of companies went under and mergers and acquisitions occurred often.

I resigned from my job in the latter half of the 1980s. It was right after the peak of the bubble. Banks were soaring because of the bubble. It is fine for a company to buy real estate out of need. It is tough to be patient and to wait when the land might become useful in the future and the prospects of the prices are rising. Seeing others make money would make you feel foolish. For example, if your next-door neighbor bought a condominium for 100 million yen [one million dollars] but becomes 200 million yen [two million dollars] the following year. The temptation to make 100 million yen without working would be great. If the bank told you to borrow money so that you can buy a condominium and you think, "I don't need a condominium now but in one year, I can make 100 million yen," you would give in to the temptation. It is very difficult to save 100 million a year. With thoughts like this, you finally give in and buy the condominium.

Companies also experienced something similar. However, the amount of money is much larger. Instead of buying a unit in a condominium, they buy the whole condominium complex. Golf was in its height in popularity and development of golf courses became popular, so companies bought land to develop golf courses. During that time, the price of golf club membership also kept going up. Golf club memberships also have a value as an asset. Many people were told that as part of their asset management they should buy golf club memberships, so they can wait for the prices to go up.

By buying and developing golf courses, companies would feel they are wasting their purchase by not using those golf courses. So they started golf as entertainment service. Many CEOs, management personnel and department heads would show up to the golf courses and play golf on the weekdays with their clients instead of working. The bubble burst after this. During this time, the media's jealousy or criticisms against corrupted company ethics came about. The feeling was to simply crush the companies. The media destroyed them like how Yemma[*] gives spirits their verdict.

After that, those who utilized their company name to eat and enjoy themselves started to realize that they could not have nightlife. The media and the public denounced that these people lacked in ethics and that company money should not be used to play. A company will sustain heavy losses if it cannot foresee these things.

Pulling out of a boom is also the work of The finance department

Furthermore, bowling alleys were a hot topic in the 1970s. There were many companies that hurt themselves by purchasing golf courses and bowling alleys.

The company I used to work for was like this, too. They hid this well — they had bought a golf course in a remote location in Hokkaido. Although they bought it, it was far away and difficult to get to. They most likely invested in it because they thought the prices would rise. However, the golf course required development expenses.

The Nasu Shoja[†] property, which our organization bought, is part of a district that was developed as a golf course. It took them 15 billion yen [150 million dollars] to develop a golf course with an area of about one million square meters. Although it took 15 billion yen to develop it, the golf craze had ended before using it even once. And it cost 50 million yen [500,000 dollars] a year just to mow the lawn. Happy Science bought this land to make effective use of it. We built Nasu Shoja and Happy Science Academy there and are utilizing the space effectively.

The seller of this land was probably happy that Happy Science was able to utilize the land instead of him needing to pay 50 million a year to mow the lawn. Trends come and go. This occurred in many places.

Golf was a trend. Bowling was a trend. There was a trend where cafés had *Space Invaders* game installed. Everyone was playing the game. There was a time when there was Space Invaders everywhere. But that particular trend did not last long. Although it was seen all across the country, it was all gone in the blink of an eye. If, during that time, the company that produced the video game knew that their time was up and left the business, they probably would not have perished. If they did not know when to leave and instead increased their production line, employed a lot of people and borrowed a lot of money to keep their business running, they probably went bankrupt with an overwhelming stock of the games.

---

* Yemma: the lord of Hell and the underworld in Buddhism and Hinduism. Also the god who judges the dead.

† The Nasu Shoja: one of the head temples of Happy Science, located in Tochigi Prefecture.

There was a time when *Tamagotchi** became popular. When Tamagotchi was selling like no other, its manufacturer built more factories to keep up with the demand. But once the trend was over, they could no longer sell Tamagotchis. This is another reason why a company fails.

Entrepreneurs must know when to pull out of a trend. If the entrepreneur cannot, the finance department must know when to pull out of a trend. The finance department will be required to decidedly say, "This trend has continued for a year. We will not be able to survive with these expanded production lines if the trend cools off, our sales become low and we are left dealing with returned merchandise." Being able to divide up the risk by shipping out a lesser amount even if the order numbers are high, or outsourcing production while halting production in your own company, is important. This is the job of the finance department. Basically, the department must do these tasks.

3

Thinking Financially as Observed in Matsushita and Nakauchi Philosophies

Differences in management as seen in Discounting vs. reasonable profits

Predicting large changes in trends and foreseeing the end of a boom require talent. In essence, these are innate abilities or talent. However, a person's talent in finance cannot be determined unless you let him try. There are cases where you must acquire knowledge and experience before your talent blossoms. Abilities in finance will also become more developed as one gains experience through things like fears of bankruptcies or economic booms.

An iconic example would be the conversation between Konosuke Matsushita[†] and Daiei's Isao Nakauchi[‡] that was later called the Kyoto Talks. Matsushita owned

---

[*] Tamagotchi: a portable game that was sold by a Japanese toy manufacturer in 1996. Became extremely popular in 1997.

[†] Konosuke Matsushita [1894-1989]: a late business manager who founded and established Matsushita Electric Industrial Company (now called Panasonic). In Japan, he is known as "the god of management." In his later years, Matsushita devoted himself to raising many politicians.

[‡] Isao Nakauchi [1922-2005]: a late Japanese business owner. Started up and expanded Daiei, one of the largest supermarket chains in Japan. Nakauchi contributed to building and establishing a consumer-based distribution through the development of Daiei.

a 6,600-square-meter Zen temple-like garden called the *Shinshin'an* and he would invite important people there and have talks. At the time, Daiei's Nakauchi was implementing a "½ Off Sale Revolution!" in all Daiei locations. He was lowering the price of products. If Daiei were to sell a TV by Matsushita Electric Industrial Company [now called Panasonic], they would need to drop the prices, too. However, Matsushita had a policy to sell products at the retail price. If Matsushita Electric could not sell at the retail price, their wholesalers would go bankrupt and any store linked with Matsushita Electric would go bankrupt. If Daiei decided to cut prices, all the customers would go there and the electronics stores under Matsushita Electric would go bust. So Konosuke Matsushita needed his products to be sold at retail price, even at Daiei. Matsushita decided to speak with Nakauchi in order to inform him of this.

Konosuke Matsushita believed in an existence of reasonable profits or fair returns. He had a philosophy of adding a reasonable profit onto expenses to calculate the retail price. Nakauchi was keeping track of American trends and sales techniques. He learned that, in America, it was popular to sell using discounts and he believed Japan would have an era of discounts as well. In America, large companies grew by cutting prices, even if that meant other smaller companies going bankrupt. Nakauchi knew this would happen in the future.

And that's not to say he was wrong. This is exactly what happened. 100-yen shops and convenience stores are popular right now. Convenience stores are challenging department stores; they have also started selling suits. It is like seeing a destroyer in an even battle against a battleship. Nakauchi saw an era of discounting in America and his guess that it would be a trend in Japan was correct.

But Matsushita was persistent, too. In order to see what wholesaler was buying Matsushita Electric products and discounting them, he added serial numbers using a kind of fluorescent lighting that could not be seen under ordinary conditions. He did so in order to track the purchase routes of the products. He tracked down which wholesaler was selling their products to Daiei at a discount and stopped them. For 30 years he continued this battle against wholesalers who were breaking the contract. In the end, both companies ended up proving valid points in their reasoning.

Konosuke Matsushita did not participate in The real estate business

The business strategy of Daiei was to buy extra land. When the land prices grew and they could use the land as collateral, they got a larger loan from the bank, bought more land and opened a large store in the suburbs. Using this store, they would use it as collateral to get the funds needed to expand their management.

The business strategy of Matsushita is, for example, as written in many books, described in a story of him building a factory after he visited a rural town in Tottori Prefecture. A female staff at a hotel asked Matsushita if he could build a factory there. The young people all leave for a larger city since there are no industries in that town. When he did build the factory, he only bought what he needed. If the factory needed 10,000 *tsubos* [1 tsubo is roughly 3.3 square meters] worth of land, he bought no more than 10,000 tsubos of land. Regularly, if a factory is built, the land surrounding the factory also goes up in price. This is why many will opt to buy 20,000 tsubos and use 10,000 tsubos for the factory. When the price of the land doubles, they could sell the extra 10,000 tsubos and offset the cost of building the factory. This means the factory was built for free. This is indeed an easy way.

The idea of free money is a temptation that you can fall for. Daiei did this, as well as Sogo [a large department store chain in Japan]. The former president and chairman of Sogo, Hiro-o Mizushima, attended Chu-o University and graduated with a doctorate. He wrote his dissertation on the idea of buying prime land in front of a train station and building a flagship store, because that will increase the price of land. Then the collateral you can use to borrow money from the bank grows, which will assist you in buying more prime locations and building more stores. However, his theory ended up backfiring. Once the bubble burst and the price of land dropped, even Sogo had difficulty staying afloat.

Earning money legitimately without trying out shortcuts to earn large profits was a thought that Mitsui and Sumitomo[*] had since the Edo period. Matsushita also thought in this way, saying, "I understand that buying more land will make me more money, but my main line of work is not in real estate. If I start making more money in real estate dealings, I would feel ridiculous trying to steadily develop and sell electronics. This is why I don't want to embrace this theory."

---

[*] Mitsui and Sumitomo: both the Mitsui clan and the Sumitomo clan are conglomerates that emerged in the beginning of the Edo period [1600s]. The two clans diversified their businesses and expanded their scale of management, transforming them into business tycoons that they are today.

In the end, Matsushita's ideas were safer. This was an old anecdote. I do not know how Panasonic is performing now, but I believe that Matsushita's strategy on real estate was better than Nakauchi's.

The limits of discounting and reasonable profits

There were some doubts as to whether or not the discounting method was correct. When I was still working for a company, I foresaw that, although Daiei's ½ Off Sale Revolution would allow them to grow as long as they have rivals to defeat, once their opponents were all defeated, they would ultimately end up crushing themselves. This is a very difficult matter to deal with.

Matsushita had a philosophy that was called "the tap water philosophy." This philosophy stated that if a company continues to supply an infinite amount of products, these would become almost free like getting water from a faucet. No one who drinks from it would be called a thief. But all products must be cheap if this philosophy was to be put into practice.

When Toshihiko Yamashita was one of the lowest executives of Matsushita Electric, he said, "The products of Matsushita Electric are not cheap at all. They are actually quite expensive." Matsushita was quite upset after hearing this.

However, later on, Matsushita promoted him 25 positions higher in the corporate ladder to make him the next CEO of the company. The words of Yamashita, who claimed that the company merchandise were expensive although Matsushita preached the tap water philosophy, was true because at Matsushita Electric, they overlay a reasonable amount of profit on top of the cost. From a discounted items standpoint, this is expensive. However, the side providing the products will obviously fall into such way of thinking. Various things similar to this happened in history of businesses.

4

What is a Sense of Finance?

Having a sense of finance means being able to Differentiate between investment and expenditure

The awareness of the management's concerns over the company's funds, property or flow of money forms part of core of management, but not the entirety of company management. I believe the finance department who supports this is considerably important. What is extremely difficult is to differentiate whether a transaction is an investment or an expense. It is almost impossible to differentiate, based on accounting principles, whether a transaction is an investment or a consumption, or an investment or an expenditure. Having sense of finance means you must be able to assess whether something is an investment or an expenditure. This is where your skill shows.

Can the company truly say that if they spend 100 million yen [one million dollars] on something right now, it will become 200 or 300 million yen [two or three million dollars]? Or will it just increase the expenditures? Will using the surplus and creating a new company just increase the expenditures or will this be an investment? It is truly difficult to tell the two apart.

If a company is profitable in some aspects of the business, many will agree with putting in more money into them. The difficulty lies in assessing whether a department that is losing money now will grow into a money tree in the future by putting more money into it.

From an accounting perspective, the departments that are in the red will most likely get cut off. However, even some businesses in the red have potential to progress in the future to become a viable business. These businesses will be in the red until they progress but will get in the black and bear fruit once it passes the threshold. Whether you can differentiate between the two would indicate whether you have management ability or sense of finance. There are departments that you should spend money on and others that you shouldn't.

A company will require experts on finance After growing past a certain point

Yesterday, I read an article on the front side of an evening paper about a company that runs vegetable factories. It is a company that was able to survive a tough competition where it is said that only one company out of ten survives. The company is currently being shown on television and written about in newspapers. The company is planning to expand by building more factories. Although this is uplifting, I would say they are approaching danger in terms of finance. The company may go bust if it does not have a well fit expert on finance. Even if the company progresses, there must be somebody looking after cost control and keeping watch to see whether the investment can return profitable results. Otherwise, it can get dangerous.

Even though there are needs for the product, there are plenty of cases where a rival that appears later on may take market share from your company or the demand for your product may be lost. This is where you must look out for danger. The management of a company becomes more difficult after it grows past a certain size. Management of the company gets dangerous when it grows over what the CEO can handle. Management will not be possible without the help of an expert on finance.

Sometimes the bank could serve as the substitute of company's finance department if it does not exist. When the company wants to expand its factory or production line, the bank can give them a loan. The company must provide paperwork and the CEO must communicate with the bank for a loan. However, banks may not give out the loan even after listening to his explanation.

In some cases, a company cannot hear an insider's opinion because the finance department is not yet trained enough. However, as an outsider's opinion, if the bank does not want to lend any money, it means that the bank sees it dangerous to give out a loan to the company.

Even if internally the company believes it will succeed, if an outsider sees risk, the company must think of why this is so. This means the company requires a more advanced skill of persuasion.

The difficulties of asset management that are Influenced by what is beyond your control

In finance, asset management is a difficult matter. There will be times when your own efforts will not be enough. For example, something like "Abenomics"[*] can start all of sudden. The economic policy of the Democratic Party of Japan [DPJ] did not work, but Abenomics followed. During the Koizumi administration [around 2005] the

---

[*]Abenomics: a neologism that comes from the combination of "Prime Minister Abe" and "economics." It is an economic policy proposed by Shinzo Abe of the Liberal Democratic Party, who formed his second cabinet in December 2012.

stock prices soared and our economy did well, however, once the DPJ came into power, most of those who had stocks as their operational strategy suffered heavy losses. These losses were never compensated for.

If fish cannot be caught due to a factory's waste or if the air gets dirty due to a nuclear accident, then compensation will be given for any loss caused by these things. But there is never compensation for the drop in stock prices caused by government policy. That is how tough this matter is.

Abenomics is doing well right now, but people are watching carefully as to where this will lead them. This is because they do not know what would happen if they ride the good economy and the administration were to change. If they could see that things won't change, that would be fine. But people are afraid the economic policies may revert back. The average stock price [Nikkei 225] is averaging 15,000 yen [150 dollars], however, if it were to revert to the 7,000 yen [70 dollars] mark, there will be huge losses. Although the government wants to raise the stock prices, no one knows whether this will actually happen, so everyone will be worried. Being able to assess the situation is very difficult. The situation becomes difficult when there are aspects beyond what you have control over or influences from foreign affairs.

Analyzing wartime consumption and risk from The standpoint of financial thinking

The Great Depression occurred in the United States in 1929. Japan also entered recession the following year [the Showa Depression]. In order to get out of this, Japanese troops advanced into Manchuria to try to mine for coal and iron ore. Recession may cause wars, too.

In general, wars cause inflation. But in some cases, wars may not stop at inflation and can lead the country to economic destruction or to ruin. Wars are quite difficult as such things do happen.

Furthermore, there are times when consumption increases in foreign countries which are waging war. By exporting to these countries, some may make a lot of money. But ironically, those countries may not be able to make payments. In that case, people could gain profit if an international financial institution can guarantee payments on behalf of the countries. But even still, there are risks involved when selling during warring periods. There are possibilities of profit but also failure. Assessing this situation is difficult as well.

During my days at the trading company, there was the war in Afghanistan. Iran and Iraq were also at war. It was a very difficult time. Anytime we exported, the paperwork would be passed through the foreign exchange department. But disturbingly, my company was exporting to both sides. We were exporting trucks for civilian use. Although the trucks were designated as civilian use, we knew that they were being used for military purposes.

Our company was selling products to the countries that were fighting each other in the war. Both of these countries would use the trucks as an alternate to tanks, where they would put people equipped with machine guns on the trucks and have them shoot at each other. If a dynamite blows up those trucks, new trucks would be necessary and there would be expenditures. We were selling trucks to both countries.

But even in this case, there is a time to withdraw. There will be a time to pack up and leave. When we know payments cannot be guaranteed, our company will have to withdraw from exporting to that country. It is also true that the time right before withdrawing is the best time to make a profit. If we continue to sell when our competitors are starting to leave, we will get more revenue. Conversely, withdrawing earlier is safer. If we withdraw too late, there would be the risk of never being able to collect for the exports; everything would go to waste. I recall our company doing a thing like this.

There was also a time when we sold a lot of trucks made in Jakarta. We sold trucks, knowing that we were selling the products to the countries that were fighting each other. Misjudging the time to withdraw would bring devastating results. If we were unable to recover the payment for the trucks, the company would have suffered a serious blow. Difficult cases like these are still happening today.

Currently, the Abe administration is trying to change their interpretation regarding the rights of collective self-defense. Prime Minister Abe is trying to make Japan be able to sell weapons internationally. There is no way to expand the defense industry without being able to sell weapons. If a country is not allowed to sell weapons, they will not be able to manufacture them. Furthermore, costs cannot be lowered unless they can be sold in larger quantities.

The government might be attempting to take military action as their ultimate inflation strategy. Although this might be so, I will not speak much more about it.

In the past there were the Korean special procurements[*]. Some wars bring about special procurements while others don't. A factory or company overseas might sustain damages. On the other hand, a company might fail to collect accounts receivable within the home country.

---

[*]Korean special procurement: during the Korean War which started in 1950, Japan experienced an economic boom as the U.S. military increased its procurements in Japan.

Furthermore, a country would send ODA[*], which are interest free, to countries that are not able to return the money. The money turns into a handout in this situation, because such countries cannot return what they don't have. In that case, the donor country does not get paid back. I believe financial thinking is necessary from country-level to company-level.

---

[*] ODA (Official Development Assistance): aid and investments donated by governments of developed countries or their agencies to developing countries for the improvement of economic development and welfare of recipient countries.

5

Debt-free Style Management And Self-help Economy

The number of companies that practice debt-free Style management is less than one in a hundred

Happy Science has constantly adhered to a debt-free style management. Happy Science is virtually over 99 percent debt-free. In the past, we borrowed some money and within these funds there was a long-term loan that we still pay back. However, for the most part we are fundamentally free of debt now. Happy Science started with no capital and has continued this style until today.

We were able to build, with no loan, two integrated middle and high schools and are currently building Happy Science University. This is mouthwatering for banks; they want to lend us money. These banks will not want to lend money to companies who want to borrow money. They want to lend money to companies who do not need to borrow money. A bank will tell a company like that to expand larger and will offer money as a loan. However, expansion is dangerous in these situations and must be dealt with carefully.

Konosuke Matsushita also mentions that there is no more than one company in a hundred that can practice debt-free style management. In Japan, over 70 percent of all companies are in the red, so there is no way there can be one in a hundred companies practicing debt-free style management. Perhaps it's less than even one in ten thousand companies.

The attitude of building own capital
Earns the trust of banks

If you want to practice debt-free style management, you cannot invest in large facilities, hire people or advertise until you have saved up a certain amount of your income to fund your company. So, in the beginning, it may seem as though your business is slow and in a perilous state.

If you borrow from the bank and start a business, you will be able to start as a company from the beginning. Companies that do so can be seen as being quick, just like the hare in *The Tortoise and the Hare*. Companies that save up money to start their business are the tortoise; they seem to take a lot of time to start up their company.

The norm in the past was to take out a loan, thinking that you can return it in about three years. Using this money, you hire people, rent an office, buy desks, start purchasing products and start up a business. You make enough profit to repay the loan within three years, return the money to the bank and make the company larger. This is how it is thought of regularly.

Let's take an entrepreneur who wants to take out a loan of 30 million yen [300,000 dollars] from a bank to start a business. The bank will obviously ask how much fund he has available at that time. Of course, the entrepreneur is taking out a loan because he does not have all of the money, so he wants to receive a loan to cover the remaining amount. He replies by saying he has five million yen [50,000 dollars]. The bank asks a follow-up question asking how he was able to come up with the five million yen. The entrepreneur might say that he raised five million from his sales and savings but required 25 million yen [250,000 dollars] more. Or he may say he borrowed five million yen from his relatives or his father, claiming that he did not save up any money on his own.

Which reply will make the bank want to lend him money? The case where he was able to save up five million yen by himself. He will be required to save 30 million yen first before starting if he wishes to practice debt-free management.

But although he may not be able to raise the entire 30 million yen by himself, the bank will trust somebody who was able to raise, more or less, some funds before starting the business. Banks trust those who are able to build up funds for themselves, who scrimped when necessary and, worked hard and efficiently to raise income.

When it comes to loaning money, those who are trusted are the ones who were able to come up with their own money or who saved up money by working a regular job. Furthermore, those who borrow from others from the get-go and do not produce their own start-up funds are suspected by banks to not have much management talent. There is a risk involved. Even if such people start a company, there is a chance that the company will go bust. Banks have a tendency to loan money to people who are able to save and build up capital, because such people can be trusted. Although a company head may not be able to practice debt-free management, banks will want to loan money to those who want to build up their own capital as much as they can.

The point is the personality. Banks look at the personalities. People who try to profit at someone else's expense are dangerous as business owners. They may be singing praises about themselves because they believe the idea they came up with will surely be a success. But objectively speaking, it can be said that whether the idea will hit or whether the idea has been thoroughly researched is questionable.

Keynesian economics is
The method to get out of recession

Nowadays, it is nearly impossible for a company to be absolutely debt-free. The truth is, with interest rates being low, it is easier to borrow money to start a company. But the reality is, not many businesses start and grow like how the government wants them to.

The low interest rates now are like a dream compared to the high interest rates ages ago. It would be very easy if one were able to grow larger using low interest rate funds; even a simple business could make profit. The fact is, you must make more profit than the bank interest in order to repay the money. Having low interest rates means business people are at an advantage. However, even with this, there are fewer people borrowing money. This means people still believe that the outlook on economy will be difficult.

I believe this is all an issue of how macroeconomics and microeconomics are understood. Keynesian economics[*] is taught at universities and is still being used by government offices today. To explain simply, Keynesian economics is not a theory that covers the whole of economics. The biggest strength of Keynesian economics lies in getting out of recession.

[*] Keynesian economics: the economic theory presented by British economist John Maynard Keynes. It advocates active government intervention in order to overcome economic recession and unemployment.

The true value of Keynesian economics could be seen in its method to escape from recession after World War I. At the time, Keynes came up with the ideas of a fiscal stimulus: getting out of recession by increasing government spending. The Japanese government is still doing this.

In general, people will revert to saving money if they believe investing their money will not produce profits in the future. They do not invest, but instead save. Consumption drops. Unemployment will naturally go up since products will not be bought. Then comes recession. Thus, fiscal stimulus will be needed to improve the economic situation. The government uses bonds or another fund to stimulate the economy. The money brings about more jobs and the unemployed are relieved. Therefore, the economy goes into an upward trend.

Once the economy goes into an upward trend, a business will grow if you invest money into it. If you buy expensive products or land, they will appreciate in value. Prices of various things will go up. People will spend money when they see this trend because their money will bear fruit.

The traps and drug-like effect Observed in Keynesian economics

If you are trying to get out of recession but people are inclined to save, then that is a dangerous situation. There needs to be a plan of action to increase consumption. And this is where the greatest contradiction lies in Keynesian economics.

"In order to get out of a short critical era, an era of a few years of recession and a large number of unemployment, it is necessary for the government to invest more money and absorb the unemployed back into businesses, even if that means the government going into the red." The idea was to create a boom with these techniques. And this idea actually gave results. This is why everything was flavored in Keynesian economics a generation ago. However, Keynes himself stipulated the drawbacks of Keynesian economics. The reason people decide to invest without saving is because they expect their investments will come back to them as a profit. This happens if they see that interest rates will go up, that there is a trend toward inflation or that prices and value of items go up.

In order to get out of recession, however, the interest rates must be lowered. Recession will continue if the interest rates are not lowered, so the government is still keeping their low interest-rate policy. It is easy to procure money if the interest rates are low, but less people invest in Japan now. This is because they think their investments will not bear fruit. They tend to save because they fear recession. They will not want to let go of their money, so they will save.

Because individuals try to save to protect their assets, the government will try to tax these assets. The government implements consumption taxes that can never be dodged. Another way the government can tax is to put a property tax, luxury tax when buying luxury goods or implement an inheritance tax. By taxing the citizens, they attempt to forcefully take the money that the citizens are saving. The government will decide to use it on behalf of the people. By using the money, a larger government will be created. As the government gets larger, so will their deficit.

The truth is, Keynesian economics is only a temporary way to get out of recession. Keynes, himself, knew this. But the flow does not stop there. During a boom cycle, the government will spend all their tax revenue and during a bust cycle, they will continue to go in debt and use money in order to counter the recession, which increases their debt. This is the continuous financial trap.

In the early half of the 1980s, the Second Administrative Reform Committee[*] led by Toshio Doko was hard at work to consolidate their finances during the Nakasone administration [1982-87]. The budget deficit during that time was 100 trillion yen [one trillion dollars] and was said to be an astronomical figure. Currently, our government deficit is one quadrillion yen [10 trillion dollars]; it has gone up tenfold. Although they tried very hard to lower their budget deficit, it is currently 10 times more than what it used to be. That is how difficult it is to deal with.

Keynesian economics, which theorizes to invest your way out of recession, is like a drug. People become numb. Once the government does it, it gets fun and hard to stop. The system has the government distribute money, which in turn wins votes and wins people's popularity. People can get jobs. Their salaries go up. This is so fun, it can't be stopped. However, the country is in the red in terms of finances. This is also the trap of democracy. How you would deal with this is a difficult problem.

---

* Second Administrative Reform Committee: committee led by Chairman Toshio Doko. Established in 1981, the committee upheld policies founded on the rebuilding of economy without increasing taxes and continued until 1983. The committee advocated cuts in spending through the revision of government organizations and the privatization of the three major public corporations (Japan National Railways, Japan Tobacco and Salt Corporation, Nippon Telegraph and Telephone).

Hayek's small government idea and The spirit of capitalism

Although not as popular during the Keynesian era, Hayek came out and opposed the idea of Keynes. Hayek stated that an economy under bureaucratic control would ultimately fail because it weakens the private sector. The private sector must voluntarily use originality and ingenuity, raise profits and make progress in their companies. This is where the fundamental idea of capitalism lies. If a person is getting work through public investment by the government, that is the same thing as being fed on a subsidy.

In terms of Hayek's economic theory, he believes in a smaller government with minimum laws. All else have the financial freedom to grow as they wish. Any business that stays alive and grows under such conditions is genuine. I believe this attitude goes well with capitalism.

We are unable to completely do away with Keynesian economics and it produces results in the short term. This is especially true in Japan because administrations change in one or two years; results must come in a short amount of time, otherwise there will be no increase in the approval ratings. These reasons are why Keynesian economics does not disappear. Fundamentally, we should be like Sontoku

Ninomiya* and save the money we make and grow it. Saving and growing money while spending frugally is the basic idea, but it is extremely difficult to accomplish this.

---

*Sontoku Ninomiya [1787-1856]: a Japanese agricultural leader and philosopher. Ninomiya was originally born into a family of peasants, but became famous after reconstructing the finances of a samurai family he served. He then went on to help restore more than 600 villages and feudal domains. Ninomiya is also known as the first person to practice capitalism in Japan.

6

The Work of the Finance Department Prevents the Company from Going Bust

A company goes bust when its top heads For luxury

I assert the idea that everything depends on the top. If the CEO is too indulgent, spends too much, is vain, desires to be famous or likes to live luxuriously, the company will go bust. If the CEO gets his company's public affairs mixed up with his personal luxury, his company will fall. It's natural for him to want to boast when a company grows to a certain extent. This kind of thing comes with his title. The people who become important within the company will also have fringe benefits and they will be able to afford more. This is the natural course of things.

However, if the company falls into a crisis where it is on the verge of going in the red or is already in the red and banks no longer loan money, then the company must cut unnecessary aspects. This is very difficult to do. A habit that has already been engrained is difficult to change, so it becomes tough to cut unnecessary parts.

If you developed the habit of playing golf with your client and developed the fear, "If I stop playing, my clients will no longer do business with me," then it will be hard for you to stop no matter how much other people tell you to. Furthermore, although I'm not sure if you would be having Geishas in Shimbashi for play or business, if you stop going to a luxurious restaurant with entertainment in Shimbashi and tell the client that you want to go to a cheaper place in Gotanda, the client may get mad.

The mass media are critical toward the luxurious entertainment but when the economy was doing well, companies ushered *Asahi Shimbun*[*] reporters back in a *haiya*[†] out of fear of getting negative reviews. Companies felt that if they did not hire a haiya, Asahi would write up negative articles about them. Other news outlets were sent home in taxis, however, Asahi would get angry if they were not sent home in a haiya. Businesses felt that if the media writes badly about their CEOs in the newspaper, the company's finances could suffer. I believe the government sector had to treat the media the same way as well.

It's probably different now, but I'm not sure because I have not experienced this. When a company has a meeting

---

[*] Asahi Shimbun: a newspaper with the second most number of copies sold in Japan. Strongly liberal.

[†] Haiya: comes from the English word, hire. It generally indicates high-class taxis.

at a high-class Japanese restaurant, with an influential media like Asahi Shimbun, the company probably provides appropriate service out of fear of being written in a bad way. The media, once they get their great welcome, would probably go easy on the company. The media expected to be offered a haiya ride home. I have heard of an incident where the media wrote a harsh article on a company because the reporter was sent home in a taxi.

Reduce debt by cutting costs that can be cut, Including entertainment expenses and idle assets

That is how the media could be. Similarly, your clients would get mad if you lower the level of entertainment you offer them. However, when you are in a financial difficulty, you must offer cheaper places for entertainment because outgoing expenses must be proportional to income and managerial departments will no longer be given a budget for entertainment expenses. So they will be required to pay out of their own pocket. Administrative departments, including human resources, general affairs, finance, accounting and secretarial departments all have a budget for entertainment expenses while the company is doing well. But once the company gets into a financial difficulty, their entertainment budget will be the first to be removed.

Then come the sales departments. In sales, at the section chief level, most have about 500,000 yen [5,000 dollars] per month to spend on entertainment. For people receiving a salary of 500,000 yen per month or higher, an allowance of 500,000 yen per month was given by their company for entertainment. In a financially difficult situation, this money will be cut by the accounting department, which will be frantic in cutting expenses. The accounting department will gradually cut these expenses, but will get into a fight with the sales department because sales believes that if its entertainment expenses are cut, it will not be able to bring in business.

Next, the idle assets will be sold off. Financial conglomerates, when they have saved up a lot of money, purchase places like reception halls. Idle assets such as these will be the next to get sold off. Our Hokkaido Shoshinkan was originally the training facility for Hokkaido Takushoku Bank's employees. It was built on premium land. We bought the facility when Takushoku Bank went under. What's more, we bought it without loan. There was a Christian church nearby who started a donation and were hoping to buy it in a year's time. The church was probably frustrated since we bought the place right after they started saving up for it. However, this was the difference in our powers, so there was nothing that could be done.

Also, Bank of Japan sold an employee recreational facility they once owned along a nice beach in Okinawa. As you can see, even BOJ sold off its assets. I don't know whether or not BOJ really needed to sell it off. Perhaps it was a public move to show the government that they are actively cutting costs. This sale by BOJ was an act of determination by the leader in the finance industry; BOJ showed their resolution to other banks and companies. Similarly, if your CEO bought a yacht and is going fishing for skipjack tuna on the weekends, the yacht should be sold off. Companies will one day be required to sell off their idle assets.

Finance and accounting need to work together and come up with many ideas. The money needed for expenses can be collected by cutting off what can be cut off. You can always shrink your debt. You can shrink your debt if you cut spending on whatever is not immediately necessary. You must cut at the 1,000 yen [10 dollars] and 10,000 yen [100 dollars] levels, if necessary, otherwise your company will collapse. Almost all companies that go bust have debt. It is difficult to go bankrupt if you have no debt. This is why companies must work hard to lessen their debt. This is another difficult job of the finance department.

Negotiating with a bank
Which will not let you repay loans

When a company gets large, it will need to take out loans from tens of banks. This is difficult to do, but repaying the loans is even more so. Banks will not let you repay the debt. Even if you were to tell the banks, "We would like to repay the debt because we no longer need the money," they will not let you do so. You would think banks would be happy to have the money repaid, but this is not the case. Banks will say that they need to pay interest to people who make deposits into their banks. Banks will go bust if they do not make more profit than the interest they need to pay. This is why being paid back is troublesome for banks. Banks will further threaten large companies by saying they will not lend out money the next time those companies require large amounts of money.

As for companies, they want to return the debt because they do not want to keep paying interest. Nevertheless, banks will say, "If you return the money now, we won't be part of the next factory you decide to build. We need to pay interest on deposits, so we need people to borrow money from us. Large accounts must continue to be borrowed from us especially during a recession, otherwise we will be in trouble." Like this, companies are provoked into borrowing money that they do not need.

What is a compensating balance?

When provoked into borrowing money that you don't need, the outcome depends on the power relationship between the company and the bank. This is where the abilities of a finance expert comes into play. Your finance department will negotiate with the bank regarding conditions of loan. They will try to lower the loan amount or try to lower the interest rate on the remaining loan amount.

Another case may be what is called, "compensating balance." Let's say that a bank loans out one billion yen [10 million dollars]. However, there are many times when the bank will not let you use all of the one billion yen. If the client is a business, the bank will loan the business one billion yen, but will tell it to leave 300 million [three million dollars] out of the one billion untouched as deposit. If the bank has more power than the business, the bank may even state in the contract that the one billion yen must be kept as deposit for half a year.

When I was working at the trading company, the bank did something similar: if we borrowed one billion yen, the bank would require us to keep 300 million out of that in our account as a time deposit. With this, the 300 million yen earns interest; however, only 700 million yen [seven million dollars] is usable from the loan. The nominal interest rate is at four percent and the real interest rate is calculated on the one billion yen that is loaned out, even though 700 million yen is all that we are allowed to use. The interest rate we actually pay would be 4 percent multiplied by 10/7 [5.71 percent].

The net out will be the full interest amount on the one billion yen less the interest earned from time deposits. Dividing this remaining amount, or the amount you must repay, by the 700 million yen would get you the real interest rate or effective interest rate. Many CEOs with a technological or sales background do not know their own effective interest rates. Furthermore, banks will lend money by only showing their nominal interest rates, saying that the interest rates are low. They need to know this.

It is better for you not to calculate true interest rates without first considering how much you can use. For example, let's say that your company has a higher profit margin than the bank. The company makes 5 percent gains whereas the bank is at 4 percent interest. You would think you have a profit margin of 1 percent. However, if the bank does not let you use some of the money, the effective interest rate could be 6 percent. If this were the case, your rate of return must exceed 6 percent. Otherwise, your business will be in the red. You might mistakenly believe that you are in the black when you are actually in the red. You must be careful as you could make a mistake here.

Balancing ratios of Long-term and short-term debts

In some cases, the interest rate of long-term loans could be in line with bonds. Many times, when you take out a five-year loan, it is linked together with a five-year maturity bond and banks will say they will not lower bond interest rates even if loan interest rates are dropping. In theory, banks do not cut interest rates. This is because they are loaning out at the rates that correspond to the level of their operations. Although this is true, it is ridiculous to keep borrowing at a high interest rate when the current interest rates are lower than before. You would not want to see high interest rates when paying back a loan for five, seven or ten years while other companies are enjoying loans at interest rates that are negligible. This is why a negotiation must take place. And this is the job of the finance department. You have to change the ratio of long-term and short-term debts by negotiating with the bank.

Those who do not know well might think that a long-term loan with a larger sum of money is a safer bet. However, long-term loans normally have a higher interest rate. The shorter, for example, one-year loan will usually have a lower rate. The finance department will calculate what the ratio of long-term and short-term loans should be, in total, to get a certain loan interest rate. Furthermore, by comparing the interest rates with the sales gains, the finance department can compare how much profit they make and see if the company is able to recoup costs. In this way, the ratio of short-term and long-term loans must be controlled by the finance department.

Lowering the percentage of indirect departments During financial restructuring

If a company requires financial restructuring, another task both finance and accounting need to accomplish is to lower the percentage of indirect departments. In other words, the company must shrink the indirect departments and expand the direct departments.

Direct departments are sales and manufacturing, in other words, the aspects of the company where things are sold or produced. Indirect departments are finance, accounting, human resources, general affairs and secretaries, which are those that stay in the headquarters.

A stable company's ratio is three to seven. Thirty percent indirect departments to seventy percent direct departments. If the company goes into financial restructuring, it will shift indirect department personnel from 30 percent to 20 percent and from 20 percent to 10 percent. Those personnel are then sent to sales.

We did this in our organization, too. We created a Member Services Department in 1991. Some headquarters staff were told to carry a backpack and sell our books. Those who performed poorly were laid off. This was a fearful experience for our staff [*laughs*].

At that time, we were renting one floor of a building for 300 million yen [three million dollars] per year in Kioi-cho. As more staff moved to work there, we had to rent a floor and a half, which amounted to 450 million yen [4.5 million dollars] per year. It was a nice building, so many staff members wanted to work there. There were a lot of people from different regions of Japan and our main headquarters became filled with staff. There were a lot of staff stationed at the headquarters, using "training" as a reason for their stay.

We had just over 1,000 staff members and, out of that, 450 were stationed at the headquarters. In terms of the ratio of direct and indirect departments, about 40 percent worked at the headquarters. These staff, since they do not interact with our members, do not contribute to revenue. This is why it's been said that companies which expand their headquarters will go bust.

Recruit Holdings Co.[*] in Japan, when it was a startup company, was said to have almost failed from building its headquarters in Ginza. I don't believe this was the sole reason but when the headquarters gets larger, a lot of indirect department personnel fill up that space. The company is more susceptible to failure when there are less people in sales. When that happens, you must get your indirect department personnel out in the field. You must shift your personnel so that there are more active staff who sell, bring in income or ask for support. This is how you would operate things within the company.

[*] Recruit Holdings Co.: a classified advertisement company started by the late Hiromasa Ezoe [1936-2013] in 1960, when he was still a university student. The company grew into a large business after extending its coverage to fields such as publishing, real estate and education.

7

Financial Thinking is Serious Business

Financial decisions must be made by "Deeds of a demon, heart of Buddha"

I have talked about methods on how to make a company grow and methods on how to retreat. The finance department deals with both of these. When the finance department, or accounting and finance departments, messes up, this will be similar to an outfielder's error in baseball; the opponent will score. If your opponent scores, you will lose. Therefore, the accounting and finance departments must not let the ball through your legs.

The finance department must strategically attack in cases where the company is in a winnable situation. The department must think about which areas to invest money in and distribute it appropriately, even if it is borrowed money from the bank. Furthermore, departments that are unprofitable must be reduced. Decisions such as reducing unprofitable departments, transferring personnel toward profitable departments and investing funds into these departments must be made with financial thinking, in a strict manner. This is indeed, "deeds of a demon, heart of

Buddha." The heart is like Buddha, wanting the company to stay alive, but the decision is like a demon, harsh and strict. Finances are similar to surgeons — they cut into bodies in hopes of keeping them alive.

There are times when you need to let The company head know

There will be times when you need to let the company head know. For example, our first director general of the finance division used to work as a local bank branch manager of the Kansai area. An incident occurred shortly after we moved to the Kioi-cho building: he knocked on my door [CEO's office] and came in. I wondered what the commotion was about. He then brought me a receipt. The receipt had the name "Ue-sama" [a polite designation for addressing someone of higher stature, which is used to avoid writing the purchaser's name on the receipt] addressed to it. The receipt was for some books I bought. He told me that the books would not be written off as a business expense because the receipt was addressed to Ue-sama and that further receipts should be addressed to "Okawa-sama [my name]." He would not write it off unless the name was exact. For a moment I thought, "How dare him!" but I realized what he said was logical. If he had knowledge on how bigger companies did things, he probably wouldn't have told me that. As long as there is trust internally, having the receipt addressed to Ue-sama would still be written off as an expense. Sometimes the tax office may not point this out as an error, either. Perhaps bank employees at the local branch level look at things in more detail. In the end, he didn't accept the receipts I had under Ue-sama as business expenses, saying that it was my fault. I remember having to pay a few thousand yen for those books [*laughs*]. I have laid out a story of being attentive to details, but this is no doubt the fundamentals of finance. Expenses must be laid out in publically acceptable ways. Like this, there are things you must speak out to your superiors on.

Being in the red is a sin for entrepreneurs

Of course, there is also the matter of balance in overall management. There are R&D needed for the future of your business, or things you are doing in order to expand the range of your business, which may seem like a waste of money. Decision on whether these things are a waste or not must be made from the standpoint of overall management. This is extremely difficult. View regarding spending that cannot be clearly determined will swing either way depending on the financial situation. When in the red, decisions to accept spending as expenses will be strict. When in the black, wider range of spending will be accepted as expenses.

For instance, Happy Science produces movies. If our movies are a profitable business, the costs of my watching movies are accepted as expenses that can be written off. However, if our movie business is not profitable, accounting will deem these actions as entertainment and will ask me to pay from my own pocket.

It is quite strict. Being in the red or being in the black will differentiate good from evil or, in accounting terms, if the purchase is an expense or not. There actually is a range of discretion, so there are things that cannot be helped. Being in the red is a sin. For business owners, crime is not the only sin; being in the red is also a sin. This is how serious the world of business is.

The basics of finance is to spend Appropriately to your income

I have introduced the outline of financial thinking. I've already talked about various topics regarding finance as a whole. The basics of finance is to spend appropriately to your income. You must increase income, but also keep expenses to a minimum. Managing a nation, in its essence, is the same.

Owners of small companies and those who have 5, 10, 20 or around 50 people in their companies will, at some point, go through what I have talked about today. It is crucial to have this knowledge in advance, learn the specifics and continue to make the company grow.

I believe today's lecture covered a general scope of finance. If there are additional things you would like to ask, I will answer them.

Chapter Two

Q&A Session

July 4, 2014
Happy Science General Headquarters, Tokyo

Questioner:
Kaoru Ota
Senior Managing Director of Happy Science
General Manager, Treasury Division

Assessing Whether an Investment Is Effective, Active and Acceptable

KAORU OTA:

I would like to thank you regarding the lecture today in which the contents could be called as the bible for the treasury department or finance department. I would like to ask you about how to make effective investments.

I learned from your teachings that spending money is more difficult than collecting it. Looking at the situation in Japan recently, we hardly see the effects of Abenomics. As economist Richard Koo points out, we are in a balance sheet recession[*], where the balance sheets of the businesses are still damaged and people are not investing. In this situation, companies are streamlining their business and cutting costs. However, I believe we will absolutely require active investments for our future progress. Please teach us how to tell whether investments are effective, active and acceptable.

Furthermore, please advise CEOs on how to find the balance between income, profit and investment strategies.

We are currently in an age Where capitalism is in a crisis

RYUHO OKAWA:

Since the 1990s, financial stability was suddenly called into question, sourcing what was called "the global standard." The idea that equity ratio of banks could not dip below a certain level [BIS Regulations[†]] became popular around the world. The truth is, this expanded the recession.

If banks want to raise their equity ratio, the amount of money extendable for loans will become lower. They will start disposing of bad debts. These things will happen if they try to improve their finances only. If banks run toward self-protection, startup companies or companies who are to

---

[*] Balance sheet recession: a type of economic recession that occurs during crashes in asset values. Companies with a poor balance sheet collectively focus on paying down debt to rebalance their finances. Therefore, even if Bank of Japan administers monetary easing, these companies do not want to borrow money to invest in infrastructure, thereby causing the economy to shrink.

[†] BIS Regulations: publicized by the Basel Committee on Banking Supervision. These standards intended for banks involved in international business to adhere to a capital adequacy ratio regulation. Many countries including Japan have adopted this capital adequacy ratio regulation.

go through trials and difficulties in order to grow will not progress. This act was a dangerous trap. The government was unable to foresee bad aspects of the change.

The current EU is dealing with the same situation. Germany is the central country of the EU. Loan condition for a country with excessive debt is the reduction of their national debt. Loans will not be extended if they do not reduce their national debt. However, the number of unemployment will grow exponentially until riots and other events occur at the stage before borrowing money, when paying down national debt. It is a difficult issue, too. Countries looking to get a loan could, before their finances improve, be under massive unemployment or virtually "dead." It is difficult to say whether this is correct or not. Capitalism is in a crisis. As I mentioned, capital will not grow unless it is directed toward creating profit.

It is important to be able to tell Whether there is a bubble or not

OKAWA:

Looking at the Meiji, Taisho, Showa and Heisei Periods of Japan, I can see a lot of things have become bigger in size. It can be said that this is a bubble but, basically, our economy has been growing larger as seen from our history. The Japanese economy is now thousands of times and tens of thousands of times greater than what it was; it's an astronomical figure. The Russo-Japanese War [1904-05] cost hundreds of millions of yen. In today's terms, winning the lottery could get you enough money to cover that. You could start the Russo-Japanese War if you win a lottery. The figures are totally different. Basically, economy tends to inflate. So, being able to differentiate whether a country's economy is in a bubble or not is important.

Abenomics is the trend right now. However, investments from the private sector have not grown much. This is why the nation is taking risks and investing. People are uneasy about the outlook on the growth of Japanese economy. Therefore, the nation is saying, "You people do not have confidence in getting enough profit to make up for your investments. Although we cannot foresee what would happen after we go bust, we will be OK until then, so we will invest on behalf of the citizens."

In addition, there is the third-party nation. China is risky, so we must shift our factories to other countries. But other countries have a lot of risk, too. In Thailand, military rule has been restored. Laos and Myanmar are considered dangerous as well as the area surrounding Indonesia.

Religious wars and guerrilla warfare are occurring in many parts of the world.

As the private sector is affected by such risks, the size of government-led investments is now becoming enormous. Just as the saying goes, "We have piped unto you, and ye have not danced," the government wants people to dance, but nobody is joining in. The government is trying hard telling the private sector that they are in a booming economy, spreading money through monetary easing policy. However, the private sector still remembers that the economy suffered a depression after the Koizumi reform [2001-06]. They continue to think, "Everything might change in a few years."

The limits of capitalistic progress as observed from The bankruptcy of Lehman Brothers

OKAWA:
Although the trend of capitalism has been that it progresses as a whole, the reality is that there are limits. This is the tough part.

The bankruptcy of Lehman Brothers in 2008 occurred because Nobel laureate-level brainiacs devised various schemes — schemes where bad debts could be concealed by being spread out everywhere. Through combining and over-leveraging* them in a complex fashion, it becomes difficult to know where these bad debts came from. The buying and selling of these bad debts established, as the origin of these debts were unknown. People then bought and sold these bad debts by breaking them up and covering up a trick.

Usually, people would not buy bad debts, however, these bad debts were grouped together with other financial products, so it became impossible to tell that those were financial products which included bad debts. Significant trust was established upon bad debts being grouped together, which was created by highly intelligent people. But in the end, the scheme collapsed. It crashed, although it was thought up by people as intelligent as Nobel laureates. This is why I think capitalism has its limits.

Popcorn expands, but only to a certain limit. The small amount of corn will expand to fill up an entire bucket of popcorn. It can expand to a certain size, but not up to

---

* Leverage: a system that allows investments to be made using borrowed capital, credit or financial instruments such as derivatives, which makes it possible for the investor to invest more money than his budget allows.

the size of the room. The hard part is assessing how much larger something can grow.

Could intelligent people pull the wool over people's eyes? Not likely. They were shuffling or allocating bad debt to other places. They were probably planning to set things back to normal once the economy recovered. They were probably planning to slide by for one to two years and wait for the economy to recover, believing the uptrend economy would come again. This is probably why they acted in that way. Nonetheless, if the economy does not recover, the company will go bust. It was unfortunate because the economy works in cycles; companies may have survived if they were able to get away just for that period of time.

There is a sad story I heard about Yamaichi Securities, where the employees were taking their savings and buying company stock in the morning of the day the firm went bankrupt. This is a sentimental story, indeed. The CEO of Yamaichi Securities apologized in an interview full of tears. Only the top four or five people of the firm probably knew that it was going bankrupt; others were in the dark. Employees who were buying company stock were trying to keep their company afloat. They never knew the company would file for bankruptcy that afternoon.

Are the investments in line With your main business?

OKAWA:

A macro level trend is very hard to read. It is good to ride the wave when the winds are favorable. But you must know how to run a business that will not crash even if the winds stop or are against you. With these things in mind, you will probably wonder if it is OK to let things go by, especially when the winds are favorable and your competitors are making money through investments. There will be times when you strongly want to invest and increase profits.

In these times of investing, the basic principle is the rule of thirds. If you have 10 billion yen [100 million dollars], you would take one-third of this. One-third goes to your savings for times in need; another third is used on necessities that are actual demands of your company. The last third, at most, is the only money you should use solely to take a speculative risk. Your company is least likely to go bankrupt if this amount is within one-third of the money you have. If you start investing more than half of it, there is a chance your company will go under. Investments should be made within the range where the company will not go under even if you were to lose all the investments.

As I mentioned earlier, it may seem unfair when your next-door neighbor buys an apartment and makes 100 million yen [one million dollars] in one year. But if you do this, you could lose sight of your main business.

When we build a branch or temple, the value of land surrounding the branch or temple goes up because it is made of beautiful, ancient Greek-style architecture. However, if we started making money from this, we will lose sight of our main work, that is, religion. Building beautiful buildings and selling those after the surrounding land goes up in value is no longer religion; this is real estate business. This is something we must not do because it diverts us from our basic mission. The thing is, you must check to see that you are following your main business.

In Japan, for example, a religion is allowed to use its land to open up preschools, parking garages or sometimes even apartment complexes. There are some things that a religion can do, as stated above. I believe these are acceptable as long as they are within the range that the general public or the followers of the religion perceives them to be acceptable.

Examining the pros and cons of a business from The perspective of public interest

OKAWA:

Let's suppose our finance [treasury] division had five billion yen [50 million dollars] in spending money. The general manager of the division might say we should build pachinko parlors within the premises of our branches in Japan because they are profitable. This way, we can have all our believers gamble at pachinko slots. All the money that our believers gamble away at other pachinko parlors can be collected at Happy Science this way. Should this happen, there will be a reaction at some point. Followers may claim that this act is wrong and the media may also criticize us. The public may chastise us, too. But if, instead, we created an NPO business to help support people in need, then that may stand as an excuse.

Currently, the government is collecting a large amount of taxes and using them for public investment. The government is building Super Levees [elevated high rise embankment to protect against floods] and is also thinking about building a casino. The casino idea is related to the matter of right or wrong. If a religion were to manage a casino, the public would be mad at us. The government is an organization that serves the public interest, so I am a little doubtful as to whether the government is allowed to manage a casino, but I can understand the feeling of trying to bring the money flowing in Hong Kong, Singapore or Las Vegas to Japan. If a casino is built, the government can tax it. The government wants to build a casino because doing so will increase tax revenue. However, the citizens may respond differently.

I am not sure how profitable casinos are. For example, the prize money of a lotto is within 50 percent of its sales. That means the ones operating the casino are guaranteed to take at least 50 percent of the sales as profit. This profit goes to the local governments and their affiliate organizations.

Horseracing and bicycle racing are usually arranged in a way that the person who places a bet loses. The person who places a bet loses, but the taxes still come in to the local government. This is when the tipster swoops in for his piece of the pie. They sell tickets saying that the ticket is a winner for sure. He, himself, should buy the ticket if it is a sure win. The reason why he doesn't buy it himself but sells it is because the ticket is not a winner [*laughs*]. He makes an excuse by saying that some of the tickets in the batch are winners. That is how tipsters make money. This is their job. Horseracing and bicycle racing bring about such secondary industries, but also have an aspect to them that disturb morals. Casinos also have the same problem.

Same can be said for drugs, which can get addicting. Drugs could be taxed and that money could be collected as government revenue. The problem is, "Is it OK for the government to continue drugging the citizens?" If, like President Obama, we believe that marijuana, alcohol and cigarettes are no different from each other in its addictiveness and health damages to the body, we would be able to acknowledge marijuana as well. Japan will not acknowledge marijuana but in America, almost half the states agree with the concept. This is a delicate matter. Are organizations with high public interest allowed to run a business on something that causes harm to the morality and sentiments of the people involved? You must make decisions based on the perspective of mission management* and you must be able to see whether the task is part of your main business. This is written in Mr. Kuki's recently published book on mission management.

---

* Mission management: management that pursues the company's mission or social contributions aside from revenue.

[Refer to Hajime Kuki, principal of Happy Science University, *Atarashiki Daigaku To Mission Keiei* (A New University and Mission Management)(Tokyo: IRH Press, 2014).]

Do not stray from the one-third investment limit And from your main business

OKAWA:

As I mentioned earlier, even if you have savings that you do not need to utilize right now, you should stop at around one-third for investments so the company does not go bust. You must look at your main business and only make investments in line with that, even if other people are making a lot of money through investments.

Happy Science bought a golf course in Nasu, but did not go into the golf business. But Church of Perfect Liberty bought a golf course near Tondabayashi [in Osaka Prefecture]. The founder loved to play golf. He said that although one day there will be a building here, he would continue playing golf until that day comes. The organization built buildings slowly, such as building over only one hole's worth of space. He bought it thinking he could enjoy playing golf there until he decides to build on top of it. This may be OK until the organization goes in the red, but they should be more careful.

The Church of World Messianity [COWM] built the MOA Museum of Art in Atami [in Shizuoka Prefecture]. I went there a long time ago and it cost 300 yen [three dollars] or so to get in. I am sure that the 300 yen was a part of their income. They most definitely collected masterpieces of the world out of self-indulgence. The amount of money it cost to collect these masterpieces were probably not equal to the entry fee. As proof, COWM borrowed 15 billion yen [150 million dollars] from a bank when they built their headquarters. If they needed a loan, that means they did not have capital in hand. They may be slightly off from their main work, but they are somehow managing as an organization. They have not grown any bigger. They will probably get tangled up in a mess if they expanded any further.

The Church of World Messianity has truth, good and beauty in their teachings. They can buy paintings and antiques if they have beauty as a part of their ideals. There are a lot of other religious organizations with beauty in their teachings who start their own museums.

This includes Soka Gakkai, owner of Fuji Arts Museum. A religious organization can buy a lot if it has beauty in its teachings and may also gain profits from those items. Once their prices go up, all you need to do is to sell them at higher prices. But a religion could stray from the main path if it is not careful.

So the important thing is to take a balanced approach and assess if the investment is accompanying your main work. There are organizations that have other businesses that are not part of their main work. However, they probably will not be accused unless they crash. You should check from an overall viewpoint of ethics whether your investment is within the allowable limit.

Produce results based on sound management

OKAWA:

Basically speaking, a sound management is the best.

Our management includes guarding what we collect as offerings. We must not let the offerings go down the drain. And we must think of how we can make back the money when using it to invest in something. We must manage in this way. We are managing the Happy Science Academy as well as other NPO-type organizations. It is true that we can manage these other businesses because the main body [Happy Science] is in a surplus. However, we must assess correctly whether the profitability of the school is due to the offerings from the religious organization or due to its own profitability. It is a big mistake to take these two as the same thing.

Regarding the school activities, there wouldn't be any problem if Happy Science believers, as a whole, can accept that a certain amount of funds from the organization will go to the school. But if the school believes that the donations from the organization are simply an income and expands the business too much, failure will follow. This is why the school must build some level of financial foundation on its own. Happy Science University could register patents from their research and development and start selling them, develop something that will bring income or have the graduates donate back to our schools once they become successful in society.

Harvard University has three trillion yen [30 billion dollars] worth of assets. The graduates must all be getting promoted higher in the working society. Harvard has their students donate back once they become successful after graduation. This is a good thing. In Happy Science Group, if students would come back and donate, there would be no funding problem even if the activities of the school do not bring enough income or if the main body has to cover for the school due to it being in the red. When students become great people and become CEOs of companies in 10 years, 20 years or 30 years, they will decide to donate back to their alma mater and therefore, the school's financial foundation will be sound.

The same can be said about the Happiness Realization Party [HRP]. HRP cannot end as a money-squandering department. Political parties, as they are in the interest of the public and are acting for the good for the country, have a limit to the amount of money — monetary aid from Happy Science — they can spend that is permissible. So, they must also build their own financial foundation.

If HRP is simply conducting activities with the money donated to Happy Science, then the members will compare HRP's "credit limit" and its work results. They will then decide whether that is permissible. There is a certain period of time in which believers are able to tolerate their donations toward Happy Science being used for HRP. I believe they will not allow that to continue if the party does not achieve a certain track record or level of accomplishment. For example, HRP must have the power to create their own system such as memberships at its local branches that will help support those who wish to become politicians. Happy Science has non-profit departments. But even so, they must have a perspective of finance — to bear fruits and achieve results.

Afterword

As the founder of Happy Science, I attained both spiritual and philosophical enlightenment. Not only that, but my background in international business development and as a management professional — a financial expert at a trading company — have been a great driving force in the progress of this religion.

Other religions also have management seminars and management training. But as I was actually a professional being trained as a management executive, my guidance on managing our organization is not just writings or text on paper. Rather, the content is very serious and heavy. This book was originally composed of lectures intended for those who would become entrepreneurs or those who are managing businesses.

I have heard that the Faculty of Economics at the University of Tokyo asks bank employees to come in and give lectures, as scholars cannot teach management and economics used in society. I believe there are excellent financial experts in banking and manufacturing industries, but society and the general public as a whole say that the best financial experts are those in trading companies.

Although a special application of the secrets of enlightenment, this book will surely become a pillar in the laws of progress and prosperity that I teach. In these pages are secrets of management revealed in depth that even P. F. Drucker[*] did not know.

> *Ryuho Okawa*
> *Founder and CEO of Happy Science Group*
> *Founder of Happy Science University*
> *August 28, 2014*

---

[*] P. F. Drucker [1909-2005]: an Austrian-born management consultant and social ecologist. His works have greatly influenced the world's entrepreneurs and CEOs. Drucker is known as the father of management.

ABOUT THE AUTHOR

Founder and CEO of Happy Science Group.

Ryuho Okawa was born on July 7th 1956, in Tokushima, Japan. After graduating from the University of Tokyo with a law degree, he joined a Tokyo-based trading house. While working at its New York headquarters, he studied international finance at the Graduate Center of the City University of New York. In 1981, he attained Great Enlightenment and became aware that he is El Cantare with a mission to bring salvation to all humankind.

In 1986, he established Happy Science. It now has members in over 165 countries across the world, with more than 700 branches and temples as well as 10,000 missionary houses around the world.

He has given over 3,450 lectures (of which more than 150 are in English) and published over 3,000 books (of which more than 600 are Spiritual Interview Series), and many are translated into 40 languages. Along with *The Laws of the Sun* and *The Laws Of Messiah*, many of the books have become best sellers or million sellers. To date, Happy Science has produced 25 movies. The original story and original concept were given by the Executive Producer Ryuho Okawa. He has also composed music and written lyrics of over 450 pieces.

Moreover, he is the Founder of Happy Science University and Happy Science Academy (Junior and Senior High School), Founder and President of the Happiness Realization Party, Founder and Honorary Headmaster of Happy Science Institute of Government and Management, Founder of IRH Press Co., Ltd., and the Chairperson of NEW STAR PRODUCTION Co., Ltd. and ARI Production Co., Ltd.

WHAT IS EL CANTARE?

El Cantare means "the Light of the Earth," and is the Supreme God of the Earth who has been guiding humankind since the beginning of Genesis. He is whom Jesus called Father and Muhammad called Allah, and is *Ame-no-Mioya-Gami*, Japanese Father God. Different parts of El Cantare's core consciousness have descended to Earth in the past, once as Alpha and another as Elohim. His branch spirits, such as Shakyamuni Buddha and Hermes, have descended to Earth many times and helped to flourish many civilizations. To unite various religions and to integrate various fields of study in order to build a new civilization on Earth, a part of the core consciousness has descended to Earth as Master Ryuho Okawa.

Alpha is a part of the core consciousness of El Cantare who descended to Earth around 330 million years ago. Alpha preached Earth's Truths to harmonize and unify Earth-born humans and space people who came from other planets.

Elohim is a part of El Cantare's core consciousness who descended to Earth around 150 million years ago. He gave wisdom, mainly on the differences of light and darkness, good and evil.

Ame-no-Mioya-Gami (Japanese Father God) is the Creator God and the Father God who appears in the ancient literature, *Hotsuma Tsutae*. It is believed that He descended on the foothills of Mt. Fuji about 30,000 years ago and built the Fuji dynasty, which is the root of the Japanese civilization. With justice as the central pillar, Ame-no-Mioya-Gami's teachings spread to ancient civilizations of other countries in the world.

Shakyamuni Buddha was born as a prince into the Shakya Clan in India around 2,600 years ago. When he was 29 years old, he renounced the world and sought enlightenment. He later attained Great Enlightenment and founded Buddhism.

Hermes is one of the 12 Olympian gods in Greek mythology, but the spiritual Truth is that he taught the teachings of love and progress around 4,300 years ago that became the origin of the current Western civilization. He is a hero that truly existed.

Ophealis was born in Greece around 6,500 years ago and was the leader who took an expedition to as far as Egypt. He is the God of miracles, prosperity, and arts, and is known as Osiris in the Egyptian mythology.

Rient Arl Croud was born as a king of the ancient Incan Empire around 7,000 years ago and taught about the mysteries of the mind. In the heavenly world, he is responsible for the interactions that take place between various planets.

Thoth was an almighty leader who built the golden age of the Atlantic civilization around 12,000 years ago. In the Egyptian mythology, he is known as god Thoth.

Ra Mu was a leader who built the golden age of the civilization of Mu around 17,000 years ago. As a religious leader and a politician, he ruled by uniting religion and politics.

ABOUT HAPPY SCIENCE

Happy Science is a global movement that empowers individuals to find purpose and spiritual happiness and to share that happiness with their families, societies, and the world. With more than 12 million members around the world, Happy Science aims to increase awareness of spiritual truths and expand our capacity for love, compassion, and joy so that together we can create the kind of world we all wish to live in.

Activities at Happy Science are based on the Principle of Happiness (Love, Wisdom, Self-Reflection, and Progress). This principle embraces worldwide philosophies and beliefs, transcending boundaries of culture and religions.

Love teaches us to give ourselves freely without expecting anything in return; it encompasses giving, nurturing, and forgiving.

Wisdom leads us to the insights of spiritual truths, and opens us to the true meaning of life and the will of God (the universe, the highest power, Buddha).

Self-Reflection brings a mindful, nonjudgmental lens to our thoughts and actions to help us find our truest selves—the essence of our souls—and deepen our connection to the highest power. It helps us attain a clean and peaceful mind and leads us to the right life path.

Progress emphasizes the positive, dynamic aspects of our spiritual growth—actions we can take to manifest and spread happiness around the world. It's a path that not only expands our soul growth, but also furthers the collective potential of the world we live in.

PROGRAMS AND EVENTS

The doors of Happy Science are open to all. We offer a variety of programs and events, including self-exploration and self-growth programs, spiritual seminars, meditation and contemplation sessions, study groups, and book events.

Our programs are designed to:
* Deepen your understanding of your purpose and meaning in life
* Improve your relationships and increase your capacity to love unconditionally
* Attain peace of mind, decrease anxiety and stress, and feel positive
* Gain deeper insights and a broader perspective on the world
* Learn how to overcome life's challenges
  ... and much more.

For more information, visit happy-science.org.

OUR ACTIVITIES

Happy Science does other various activities to provide support for those in need.

◆ **You Are An Angel! General Incorporated Association**

Happy Science has a volunteer network in Japan that encourages and supports children with disabilities as well as their parents and guardians.

◆ **Never Mind School for Truancy**

At 'Never Mind,' we support students who find it very challenging to attend schools in Japan. We also nurture their self-help spirit and power to rebound against obstacles in life based on Master Okawa's teachings and faith.

◆ **"Prevention Against Suicide" Campaign since 2003**

A nationwide campaign to reduce suicides; over 20,000 people commit suicide every year in Japan. "The Suicide Prevention Website-Words of Truth for You-" presents spiritual prescriptions for worries such as depression, lost love, extramarital affairs, bullying and work-related problems, thereby saving many lives.

◆ **Support for Anti-bullying Campaigns**

Happy Science provides support for a group of parents and guardians, Network to Protect Children from Bullying, a general incorporated foundation launched in Japan to end bullying, including those that can even be called a criminal offense. So far, the network received more than 5,000 cases and resolved 90% of them.

◆ **The Golden Age Scholarship**

This scholarship is granted to students who can contribute greatly and bring a hopeful future to the world.

◆ **Success No.1**
Buddha's Truth Afterschool Academy

Happy Science has over 180 classrooms throughout Japan and in several cities around the world that focus on afterschool education for children. The education focuses on faith and morals in addition to supporting children's school studies.

◆ **Angel Plan V**

For children under the age of kindergarten, Happy Science holds classes for nurturing healthy, positive, and creative boys and girls.

◆ **Future Stars Training Department**

The Future Stars Training Department was founded within the Happy Science Media Division with the goal of nurturing talented individuals to become successful in the performing arts and entertainment industry.

◆ **NEW STAR PRODUCTION Co., Ltd.**
ARI Production Co., Ltd.

We have companies to nurture actors and actresses, artists, and vocalists. They are also involved in film production.

CONTACT INFORMATION

Happy Science is a worldwide organization with branches and temples around the globe. For a comprehensive list, visit the worldwide directory at *happy-science.org*. The following are some of the many Happy Science locations:

UNITED STATES AND CANADA

New York
79 Franklin St., New York, NY 10013, USA
Phone: 1-212-343-7972
Fax: 1-212-343-7973
Email: ny@happy-science.org
Website: happyscience-usa.org

New Jersey
66 Hudson St., #2R, Hoboken, NJ 07030, USA
Phone: 1-201-313-0127
Email: nj@happy-science.org
Website: happyscience-usa.org

Chicago
2300 Barrington Rd., Suite #400,
Hoffman Estates, IL 60169, USA
Phone: 1-630-937-3077
Email: chicago@happy-science.org
Website: happyscience-usa.org

Florida
5208 8th St., Zephyrhills, FL 33542, USA
Phone: 1-813-715-0000
Fax: 1-813-715-0010
Email: florida@happy-science.org
Website: happyscience-usa.org

Atlanta
1874 Piedmont Ave., NE Suite 360-C
Atlanta, GA 30324, USA
Phone: 1-404-892-7770
Email: atlanta@happy-science.org
Website: happyscience-usa.org

San Francisco
525 Clinton St.
Redwood City, CA 94062, USA
Phone & Fax: 1-650-363-2777
Email: sf@happy-science.org
Website: happyscience-usa.org

Los Angeles
1590 E. Del Mar Blvd., Pasadena, CA
91106, USA
Phone: 1-626-395-7775
Fax: 1-626-395-7776
Email: la@happy-science.org
Website: happyscience-usa.org

Orange County
16541 Gothard St. Suite 104
Huntington Beach, CA 92647
Phone: 1-714-659-1501
Email: oc@happy-science.org
Website: happyscience-usa.org

San Diego
7841 Balboa Ave. Suite #202
San Diego, CA 92111, USA
Phone: 1-626-395-7775
Fax: 1-626-395-7776
E-mail: sandiego@happy-science.org
Website: happyscience-usa.org

Hawaii
Phone: 1-808-591-9772
Fax: 1-808-591-9776
Email: hi@happy-science.org
Website: happyscience-usa.org

Kauai
3343 Kanakolu Street, Suite 5
Lihue, HI 96766, USA
Phone: 1-808-822-7007
Fax: 1-808-822-6007
Email: kauai-hi@happy-science.org
Website: happyscience-usa.org

Toronto

845 The Queensway
Etobicoke, ON M8Z 1N6, Canada
Phone: 1-416-901-3747
Email: toronto@happy-science.org
Website: happy-science.ca

Vancouver

#201-2607 East 49th Avenue,
Vancouver, BC, V5S 1J9, Canada
Phone: 1-604-437-7735
Fax: 1-604-437-7764
Email: vancouver@happy-science.org
Website: happy-science.ca

INTERNATIONAL

Tokyo

1-6-7 Togoshi, Shinagawa,
Tokyo, 142-0041, Japan
Phone: 81-3-6384-5770
Fax: 81-3-6384-5776
Email: tokyo@happy-science.org
Website: happy-science.org

Seoul

74, Sadang-ro 27-gil,
Dongjak-gu, Seoul, Korea
Phone: 82-2-3478-8777
Fax: 82-2-3478-9777
Email: korea@happy-science.org
Website: happyscience-korea.org

London

3 Margaret St.
London, W1W 8RE United Kingdom
Phone: 44-20-7323-9255
Fax: 44-20-7323-9344
Email: eu@happy-science.org
Website: www.happyscience-uk.org

Taipei

No. 89, Lane 155, Dunhua N. Road,
Songshan District, Taipei City 105, Taiwan
Phone: 886-2-2719-9377
Fax: 886-2-2719-5570
Email: taiwan@happy-science.org
Website: happyscience-tw.org

Sydney

516 Pacific Highway, Lane Cove North,
2066 NSW, Australia
Phone: 61-2-9411-2877
Fax: 61-2-9411-2822
Email: sydney@happy-science.org

Kuala Lumpur

No 22A, Block 2, Jalil Link Jalan Jalil
Jaya 2, Bukit Jalil 57000,
Kuala Lumpur, Malaysia
Phone: 60-3-8998-7877
Fax: 60-3-8998-7977
Email: malaysia@happy-science.org
Website: happyscience.org.my

Sao Paulo

Rua. Domingos de Morais 1154,
Vila Mariana, Sao Paulo SP
CEP 04010-100, Brazil
Phone: 55-11-5088-3800
Email: sp@happy-science.org
Website: happyscience.com.br

Kathmandu

Kathmandu Metropolitan City,
Ward No. 15, Ring Road, Kimdol,
Sitapaila Kathmandu, Nepal
Phone: 977-1-427-2931
Email: nepal@happy-science.org

Jundiai

Rua Congo, 447, Jd. Bonfiglioli
Jundiai-CEP, 13207-340, Brazil
Phone: 55-11-4587-5952
Email: jundiai@happy-science.org

Kampala

Plot 877 Rubaga Road, Kampala
P.O. Box 34130 Kampala, UGANDA
Phone: 256-79-4682-121
Email: uganda@happy-science.org

ABOUT HAPPINESS REALIZATION PARTY

The Happiness Realization Party (HRP) was founded in May 2009 by Master Ryuho Okawa as part of the Happy Science Group. HRP strives to improve the Japanese society, based on three basic political principles of "freedom, democracy, and faith," and let Japan promote individual and public happiness from Asia to the world as a leader nation.

1) Diplomacy and Security: Protecting Freedom, Democracy, and Faith of Japan and the World from China's Totalitarianism

Japan's current defense system is insufficient against China's expanding hegemony and the threat of North Korea's nuclear missiles. Japan, as the leader of Asia, must strengthen its defense power and promote strategic diplomacy together with the nations which share the values of freedom, democracy, and faith. Further, HRP aims to realize world peace under the leadership of Japan, the nation with the spirit of religious tolerance.

2) Economy: Early economic recovery through utilizing the "wisdom of the private sector"

Economy has been damaged severely by the novel coronavirus originated in China. Many companies have been forced into bankruptcy or out of business. What is needed for economic recovery now is not subsidies and regulations by the government, but policies which can utilize the "wisdom of the private sector."

For more information, visit en.hr-party.jp

HAPPY SCIENCE ACADEMY JUNIOR AND SENIOR HIGH SCHOOL

Happy Science Academy Junior and Senior High School is a boarding school founded with the goal of educating the future leaders of the world who can have a big vision, persevere, and take on new challenges.

Currently, there are two campuses in Japan; the Nasu Main Campus in Tochigi Prefecture, founded in 2010, and the Kansai Campus in Shiga Prefecture, founded in 2013.

Nasu Main Campus

Kansai Campus

HAPPY SCIENCE UNIVERSITY

THE FOUNDING SPIRIT AND THE GOAL OF EDUCATION

Based on the founding philosophy of the university, "Exploration of happiness and the creation of a new civilization," education, research and studies will be provided to help students acquire deep understanding grounded in religious belief and advanced expertise with the objectives of producing "great talents of virtue" who can contribute in a broad-ranging way to serve Japan and the international society.

FACULTIES

Faculty of human happiness

Students in this faculty will pursue liberal arts from various perspectives with a multidisciplinary approach, explore and envision an ideal state of human beings and society.

Faculty of successful management

This faculty aims to realize successful management that helps organizations to create value and wealth for society and to contribute to the happiness and the development of management and employees as well as society as a whole.

Faculty of future creation

Students in this faculty study subjects such as political science, journalism, performing arts and artistic expression, and explore and present new political and cultural models based on truth, goodness and beauty.

Faculty of future industry

This faculty aims to nurture engineers who can resolve various issues facing modern civilization from a technological standpoint and contribute to the creation of new industries of the future.

ABOUT HS PRESS

HS Press is an imprint of IRH Press Co., Ltd. IRH Press Co., Ltd., based in Tokyo, was founded in 1987 as a publishing division of Happy Science. IRH Press publishes religious and spiritual books, journals, magazines and also operates broadcast and film production enterprises. For more information, visit *okawabooks.com*.

Follow us on:

f Facebook: Okawa Books   🅾 Instagram: OkawaBooks

▶ Youtube: Okawa Books   🐦 Twitter: Okawa Books

𝓟 Pinterest: Okawa Books   **g** Goodreads: Ryuho Okawa

——— **NEWSLETTER** ———

To receive book related news, promotions and events, please subscribe to our newsletter below.

∞ eepurl.com/bsMeJj

 ——— **AUDIO / VISUAL MEDIA** ———

YOUTUBE

PODCAST

Introduction of Ryuho Okawa's titles; topics ranging from self-help, current affairs, spirituality, religion, and the universe.

BOOKS BY RYUHO OKAWA

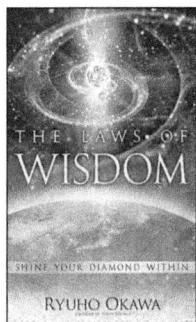

THE LAWS OF WISDOM
Shine Your Diamond Within

This book guides you along the path on how to acquire wisdom, so that you can break through any wall you are facing or will confront in your life or in your business. You will lean how to go beyond the level of just amassing knowledge. It will help you come up with many great ideas, make effective planning and strategy and develop your leadership skills.

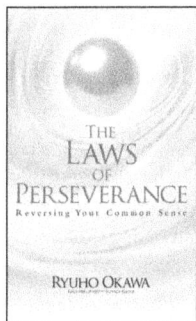

THE LAWS OF PERSEVERANCE
Reversing Your Common Sense

"No matter how much you suffer, the Truth will gradually shine forth as you continue to endure hardships. Therefore, simply strengthen your mind and keep making constant efforts in times of endurance, however ordinary they may be. "

-From the Postscript

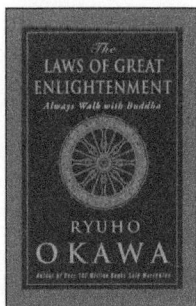

THE LAWS OF GREAT ENLIGHTENMENT
Always Walk with Buddha

We often find ourselves unable to forgive someone and maintain a peaceful mind. However, there are ways to lead a stress-free life and enjoy happiness from within. By understanding the Buddhist concept of "enlightenment" in this book, you will gain the power to forgive sins and get to know how to be the master of your own mind.

For a complete list of books, visit okawabooks.com

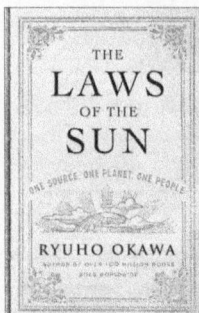

THE LAWS OF THE SUN
ONE SOURCE, ONE PLANET, ONE PEOPLE

Imagine if you could ask God why He created this world and what spiritual laws He used to shape us—and everything around us. If we could understand His designs and intentions, we could discover what our goals in life should be and whether our actions move us closer to those goals or farther away.

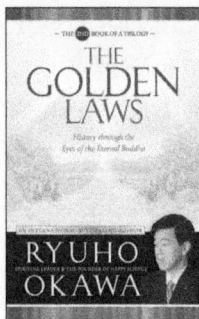

THE GOLDEN LAWS
HISTORY THROUGH THE EYES OF THE ETERNAL BUDDHA

The Golden Laws reveals how Buddha's Plan has been unfolding on earth, and outlines five thousand years of the secret history of humankind. Once we understand the true course of history, we cannot help but become aware of the significance of our spiritual mission in the present age.

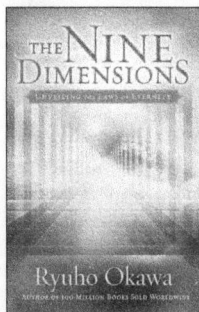

THE NINE DIMENSIONS
UNVEILING THE LAWS OF ETERNITY

This book is a window into the mind of our loving God, who encourages us to grow into greater angels. It reveals His deepest intentions, answering the timely question of why He conceived such a colorful medley of religions, philosophies, sciences, arts, and other forms of expression.

For a complete list of books, visit okawabooks.com

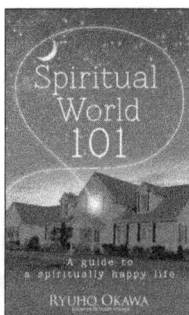

SPIRITUAL WORLD 101

A GUIDE TO A SPIRITUALLY HAPPY LIFE

This book is a spiritual guidebook that will answer all your questions about the spiritual world, with illustrations and diagrams explaining about your guardian spirit and the secrets of God and Buddha. By reading this book, you will be able to understand the true meaning of life and find happiness in everyday life.

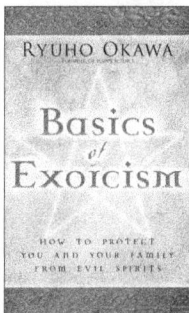

BASICS OF EXORCISM

HOW TO PROTECT YOU AND YOUR FAMILY FROM EVIL SPIRITS

This book reveals the truth regarding spiritual disturbance and the technique to cope with demons and evil spirits. No matter how much time progresses, demons are real. The essence of exorcism as a result of more than 5000 rounds of exorcist experience!

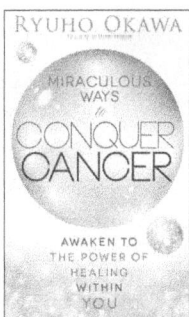

MIRACULOUS WAYS TO CONQUER CANCER

AWAKEN TO THE POWER OF HEALING WITHIN YOU

Why do people get cancer? Why does the number of patients with cancer keep increasing in spite of medical progress? This book reveals how the mind creates cancer and the keys to overcome illnesses. Drive out cancer from your life!

For a complete list of books, visit okawabooks.com

MUSIC BY RYUHO OKAWA

El Cantare Ryuho Okawa Original Songs

A song celebrating Lord God

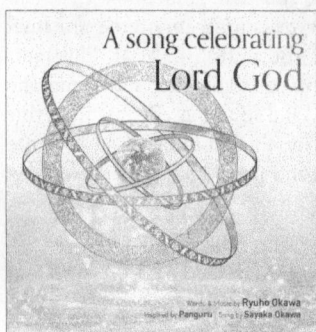

A song celebrating Lord God,
the God of the Earth,
who is beyond a prophet.

DVD
CD

The Water Revolution

English and Chinese version

For the truth and happiness of
the 1.4 billion people in China
who have no freedom. Love,
justice, and sacred rage of God
are on this melody that will
give you courage to fight to
bring peace.

DVD

CD

With Savior *English version*

This is the message of hope to the modern people who are living in the midst of the Coronavirus pandemic, natural disasters, economic depression, and other various crises.

Search on YouTube

with savior 🔍 for a short ad!

The Thunder

a composition for repelling the Coronavirus

We have been granted this music from our Lord. It will repel away the novel Coronavirus originated in China. Experience this magnificent powerful music.

Search on YouTube

the thunder composition 🔍

for a short ad!

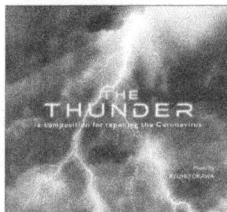

The Exorcism

prayer music for repelling Lost Spirits

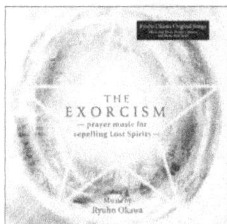

Feel the divine vibrations of this Japanese and Western exorcising symphony to banish all evil possessions you suffer from and to purify your space!

Search on YouTube

the exorcism repelling 🔍

for a short ad!

Listen now today!

🎧 Download from
Spotify iTunes Amazon

DVD, CD available at amazon.com, and Happy Science locations worldwide